SPROTT-SHAW INTERNATIONAL
LANGUAGE COLLEGE

NorthStar

READING AND WRITING

Intermediate

P9-DXS-966

SECOND EDITION

Laurie Barton
Carolyn Dupaquier Sardinas

Series Editors
Frances Boyd
Carol Numrich

Longman

NorthStar: Reading and Writing, Intermediate, Second Edition

© 2004, 1998 by Pearson Education, Inc.
All rights reserved.
No part of this publication may be reproduced,
stored in a retrieval system, or transmitted
in any form or by any means, electronic, mechanical,
photocopying, recording, or otherwise,
without the prior permission of the publisher.

Pearson Education, 10 Bank Street, White Plains, NY 10606

Development director: Penny Laporte
Project manager: Debbie Sistino
Development editors: Deborah Lazarus, Stacey Hunter
Vice president, director of design and production: Rhea Banker
Executive managing editor: Linda Moser
Production editor: Marc Oliver
Production manager: Liza Pleva
Production coordinator: Melissa Leyva
Director of manufacturing: Patrice Fraccio
Senior manufacturing buyer: Dave Dickey
Photo research: Aerin Csigay
Cover design: Rhea Banker
Cover art: Detail of Der Rhein bei Duisburg, 1937, 145(R 5) Rhine near
    Duisburg 19 × 27.5 cm; water-based on cardboard; The Metropolitan
    Museum of Art, N.Y. The Berggruen Klee Collection, 1984. (1984.315.56)
    Photograph © 1985 The Metropolitan Museum of Art. © 2003 Artists
    Rights Society (ARS), New York / VG Bild-Kunst, Bonn
Text design: Quorum Creative Services
Text composition: ElectraGraphics, Inc.
Text font: 11/13 Sabon
Illustration credits: see page 195
Photo credits: see page 195
Text credits: see page 195

**Der Rhein bei Duisburg
Paul Klee**

Library of Congress Cataloging-in-Publication Data

Barton, Laurie
    NorthStar. Reading and Writing, intermediate / Laurie Barton, Carolyn
Dupaquier Sardinas.—2nd ed.
        p. cm.
    Includes index.
    1. English language—Textbooks for foreign speakers. 2. English
language—Rhetoric—Problems, exercises, etc. 3. Report writing—Problems,
exercises, etc. 4. Reading—Problems, exercises, etc. I. Title: Reading and
writing, intermediate. II. Sardinas, Carolyn Dupaquier III. Title.

PE1128.B54 2003
808'.0427—dc21

2003044729

ISBN: 0-201-75571-8 (Student Book)
       0-13-184675-2 (Student Book with Audio CD)

LONGMAN ON THE **WEB**

Longman.com offers online resources for
teachers and students. Access our Companion
Websites, our online catalog, and our local
offices around the world.

Visit us at **longman.com.**

Printed in the United States of America
15 16—CRK—11 10 09 08
8 9 10—CRK—09 08

Contents

Welcome to NORTHSTAR

Second Edition

NorthStar leads the way in integrated skills series. The Second Edition remains an innovative, five-level series written for students with academic as well as personal language goals. Each unit of the thematically linked Reading and Writing strand and Listening and Speaking strand explores intellectually challenging, contemporary themes to stimulate critical thinking skills while building language competence.

Four easy to follow sections—Focus on the Topic, Focus on Reading/Focus on Listening, Focus on Vocabulary, and Focus on Writing/Focus on Speaking— invite students to focus on the process of learning through **NorthStar**.

Thematically Based Units

NorthStar engages students by organizing language study thematically. Themes provide stimulating topics for reading, writing, listening, and speaking.

Extensive Support to Build Skills for Academic Success

Creative activities help students develop language-learning strategies, such as predicting and identifying main ideas and details.

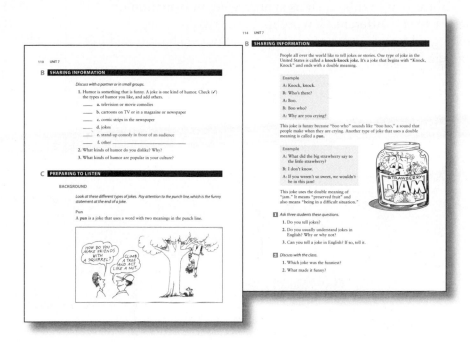

High-Interest Listening and Reading Selections

The two listening or reading selections in each unit present contrasting viewpoints to enrich students' understanding of the content while building language skills.

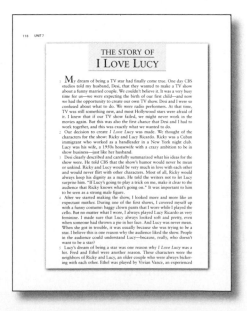

Critical Thinking Skill Development

Critical thinking skills, such as synthesizing information or reacting to the different viewpoints in the two reading or listening selections, are practiced throughout each unit, making language learning meaningful.

Extensive Vocabulary Practice

Students are introduced to key, contextualized vocabulary to help them comprehend the listening and reading selections. They also learn idioms, collocations, and word forms to help them explore, review, play with, and expand their spoken and written expression.

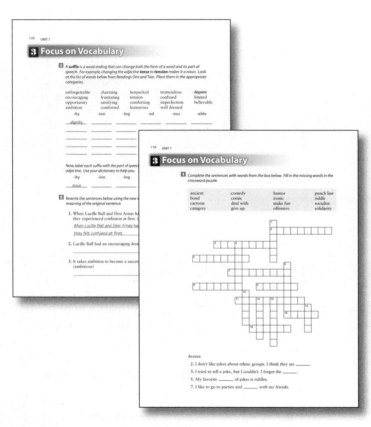

Powerful Pronunciation Practice

A carefully designed pronunciation syllabus in the Listening and Speaking strand focuses on topics such as stress, rhythm, and intonation. Theme-based pronunciation practice reinforces the vocabulary and content of the unit.

Content-Rich Grammar Practice

Each thematic unit integrates the study of grammar with related vocabulary and cultural information. The grammatical structures are drawn from the listening or reading selections and offer an opportunity for students to develop accuracy in speaking or writing about the topic.

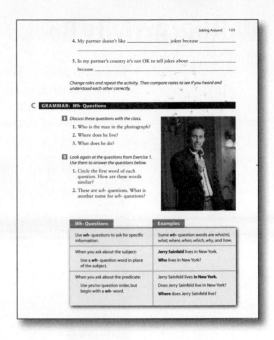

Extensive Opportunity for Discussion and Writing

Challenging and imaginative speaking activities, writing topics, and research assignments allow students to apply the language, grammar, style, and content they've learned.

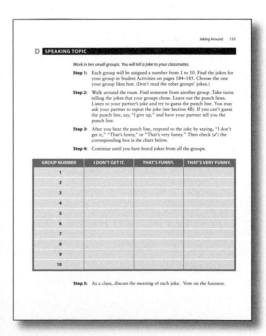

Writing Activity Book

The companion *Writing Activity Book* leads students through the writing process with engaging writing assignments. Skills and vocabulary from **NorthStar: Reading and Writing,** are reviewed and expanded as students learn the process of prewriting, organizing, revising, and editing.

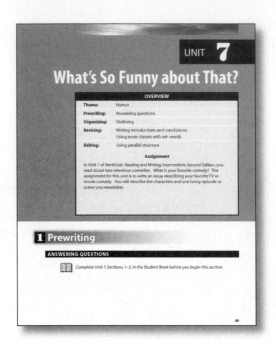

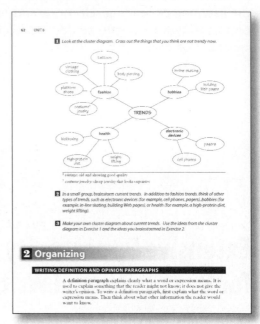

Audio Program

All the pronunciation, listening, and reading selections have been professionally recorded. The audio program includes audio CDs as well as audio cassettes.

Teacher's Manual with Achievement Tests

Each book in the series has an accompanying *Teacher's Manual* with step-by-step teaching suggestions, time guidelines, and expansion activities. Also included in each *Teacher's Manual* are reproducible unit-by-unit tests. The Listening and Speaking strand tests are recorded on CD and included in the *Teacher's Manual*. Packaged with each *Teacher's Manual* for the Reading and Writing strand is a TestGen CD-ROM that allows teachers to create and customize their own **NorthStar** tests. Answer Keys to both the Student Book and the Tests are included, along with a unit-by-unit word list of key vocabulary.

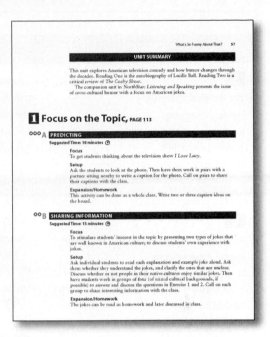

NorthStar Video Series

Engaging, authentic video clips, including cartoons, documentaries, interviews, and biographies correlate to the themes in **NorthStar.** There are four videos, one for each level of **NorthStar,** Second edition, containing 3- to 5- minute segments for each unit. Worksheets for the video can be found on the **NorthStar** Companion Website.

Companion Website

http://www.longman.com/northstar includes resources for students and teachers such as additional vocabulary activities, Web-based links and research, video worksheets, and correlations to state standards.

Scope and Sequence

Unit	Critical Thinking Skills	Reading Tasks

1
 	
The World of Advertising
 	
Theme: Advertising
 	
Reading One: *Advertising All Over the World*
    A magazine article
 	
Reading Two: *Changing World Markets*
    An excerpt from a speech
	Compare personal buying habits
	Identify and later reevaluate assumptions
	Infer information not explicit in the texts
	Connect themes between texts
	Compare and contrast advertising campaigns
		Make predictions
		Identify main ideas
		Read for details
		Support answers with evidence from the texts
		Relate information in the text to life experience
		Research local advertising campaigns

2
 	
Going to Extremes: Sports and Obsession
 	
Theme: Extreme Sports
 	
Reading One: *Interview with Tony Hawk*
    An interview with a professional skateboarder
 	
Reading Two: *High School Star Hospitalized for Eating Disorder*
    A newspaper report
	Identify personal habits and attitudes
	Compare and contrast information gathered in a survey
	Infer meaning not explicit in text
	Analyze advantages and disadvantages of athletic obsession at an early age
	Compare and contrast two figures from two texts
	Interpret character motivation
	Draw conclusions based on information in the text
		Make predictions
		Read for main ideas
		Scan for details
		Underline important information in the text
		Relate text to personal experiences

3
 	
Miracle Cure?
 	
Theme: Fraud
 	
Reading One: *A Miracle Cure?*
    A magazine article
 	
Reading Two: *The Organic Health Center*
    An advertisement
	Analyze an advertisement
	Make judgments
	Evaluate information according to criteria set forth in a text
	Correlate information from two texts
	Compare and contrast medical treatments
	Critique advertisements
		Make predictions
		Read for main ideas
		Locate information in a text
		Support answers with evidence from the text
		Read for details
		Relate supporting details to main ideas
		Summarize the readings

4
 	
The Metamorphosis
 	
Theme: Storytelling
 	
Reading One: *The Metamorphosis*
    An abridged story
 	
Reading Two: *Ungeziefer*
    A critique of the story
	Recognize personal assumptions
	Infer word meaning from context
	Examine symbol and imagery in a text
	Contrast different points of view in a text
	Interpret characters' emotions
		Make predictions
		Paraphrase main ideas
		Support answers with information from the text
		Connect generalizations to specific passages
		Locate information in the text
		Compare personal reactions to a critique
		Retell a short story with an illustration
		Research the metamorphosis process

Writing Tasks	Vocabulary	Grammar
Write a paragraph with a topic sentence, supporting details, and a concluding sentence Write a letter in response to a speech Write a commercial Describe a product Compile data with a graphic organizer	Word definitions Context clues Synonyms Idioms	Contrast simple present and present progressive
Write a factual report Write a personal reflection using new vocabulary Write an opinion response Compose interview questions Summarize interview in a factual report	Context clues Word forms Synonyms Vocabulary categorization	Modals of ability
Compose a summary paragraph Organize information within a paragraph Write topic sentences Identify and use transitions in a paragraph Report information gathered in an interview Write an advertisement Summarize research findings	Word definitions Context clues Prefixes and suffixes	Superlative adjectives
Paraphrase sentences Write statements of purpose Compose a short story Write an opinion paragraph Paraphrase research in a report and use a diagram to relate facts	Word definitions Synonyms Context clues Comparison and contrast of word meaning and usage	Infinitives of purpose Relative pronouns

Unit	Critical Thinking Skills	Reading Tasks
5 **Speaking of Gender** Theme: Language Reading One: *Different Ways of Talking* An article Reading Two: *Speaking of Gender* An interview with a linguist	Assess gender-typing in own culture Identify personal assumptions about gender Infer information not explicit in the text Support a personal opinion with examples from the text Evaluate speech according to a criteria set forth in a text Synthesize information from two readings Analyze gender influence in speech and behavior	Make predictions Read for main ideas Locate details in the text Relate text to one's own observations
6 **Ecotourism** Theme: Tourism Reading One: *Tourists in a Fragile Land* An opinion essay Reading Two: *A Travel Journal* An account of a trip to Antarctica	Compare travel experiences Test assumptions about Antarctica Infer information not explicit in the text Analyze an author's argument Hypothesize another's point of view Compare and contrast points of view from two different texts Analyze relationships between words	Make predictions Identify chronology in a text Read for details Paraphrase main ideas Relate texts to personal opinions Research ecotourism
7 **What's So Funny about That?** Theme: Humor Reading One: *The Story of I Love Lucy* An autobiographical account Reading Two: *Cosby: A Different Kind of Family Show* A TV show review	Interpret a photograph Explain the double meaning of a joke Analyze how humor reflects social and cultural values Compare and contrast characters, gender roles, and types of comedy Hypothesize another's point of view	Make predictions Identify main ideas Locate information in a text Identify supporting details Recognize the organization of a text Compare and contrast information from two texts Research a comedy star
8 **Always in Fashion** Theme: Fashion Reading One: *The Search for Beauty* A passage on plastic surgery Reading Two: *My Wife Wants to Look Younger* An excerpt from a journal	Compare assumptions and values about beauty Draw conclusions Interpret word usage Infer information not explicit in the text Hypothesize another's point of view Synthesize information from two texts Make recommendations using information from the texts Analyze cause and effect Analyze trends in fashion	Make predictions Interpret a timeline Locate main ideas in the text Read for details Connect texts to personal interests, experiences, and values

Writing Tasks	Vocabulary	Grammar
Write sentences with transitions to compare and contrast Write requests in correspondence Compose paragraphs to compare and contrast gender roles and behavior Take observation notes of a TV program Write a paragraph summary of research findings	Synonyms Context clues Vocabulary classification	Using modals for requests
Write an opinion essay Analyze use of a thesis statement, supporting details, and concluding statement in an essay Take notes in outline form Compose information questions Write a letter requesting information	Paraphrasing meaning Context clues Word associations Analogies Synonyms and antonyms	Past progressive and simple past
Use parallel structure to combine sentences Write a TV show review using parallel structure Paraphrase a text Summarize the readings using new vocabulary Summarize a dialogue using noun clauses Write a biography of a comedy star	Context clues Word definitions Suffixes Word forms Vocabulary classification	Noun clauses with *wh-* words
Write opinion statements using new vocabulary Write a persuasive letter Use transitions to show cause and effect Write a narrative in the past Summarize an interview in a paragraph Write a passage using the past tenses Report research findings on department store merchandise	Word definitions Word association	Describing the past with *used to*

Unit	Critical Thinking Skills	Reading Tasks
9 **Crime and Punishment** Theme: Punishment Reading One: *Life in Prison Is Still Life: Why Should a Killer Live? Why Do We Kill People to Show That Killing People Is Wrong?* Two newspaper op-ed articles Reading Two: *Graphs* Statistics on the death penalty	Distinguish arguments for and against capital punishment Compare and contrast punishment practices in different cultures Identify an author's point of view Hypothesize an author's values based on information in the text Interpret bar graphs and a pie chart Draw conclusions Correlate examples with abstractions	Make predictions Identify supporting ideas in an argument Relate supporting details to main ideas Identify contrasting arguments Research a country's use of capital punishment
10 **Finding a Spouse** Theme: Marriage Reading One: *Finding a Spouse* An anthropological article Reading Two: *What's Wrong with Tradition?* A letter to the editor	Identify personal assumptions about marriage Classify information Identify underlying cultural values Evaluate information in the text according to personal beliefs Rank cultural practices according to a continuum Analyze relationships between words	Make predictions Identify main ideas Read for details Research media coverage of courtship and marriage

Writing Tasks	Vocabulary	Grammar
Support opinions with facts and data Write an opinion paragraph using new vocabulary Compose complex and compound sentences Edit a passage to vary sentence structure Write a letter to the editor Write a report on research	Context clues Word definitions Abstract nouns Appropriate word usage	Contrast: present perfect and present perfect progressive
Write an opinion paragraph Write a letter stating an opinion Describe a cultural tradition of courtship Use related word forms for cohesion Summarize research findings	Word definitions Analogies Synonyms and antonyms Word forms	Articles: definite and indefinite

Acknowledgments

I dedicate this book to the ESL students and faculty at Orange Coast College.

Laurie Barton

Many people helped in the creative process that resulted in this book. I am grateful to Allen Ascher, who gave us this opportunity. I would also like to thank our colleagues at the American Language Program, California State University, Fullerton for piloting units and contributing their helpful ideas. To Debbie Lazarus and Debbie Sistino, who provided clear direction and guidance, many thanks. Most importantly, I want to express my deep appreciation to our editor, Carol Numrich. Her keen insight, her understanding of what students need, and her grace throughout the process will never be forgotten. Finally, many thanks to Luis Sardinas, Pete Dupaquier, and Carolyn Reno. Their many, many hours of support and babysitting were invaluable to the success of this project.

Carolyn Dupaquier Sardinas

For the comments and insights they graciously offered to help shape the direction of the Second Edition of *NorthStar*, the publisher would like to thank all our **reviewers**. For a complete list of reviewers and institutions, see page 197.

The World of Advertising

1 Focus on the Topic

A PREDICTING

Look at the photograph, and discuss these questions with the class.

1. What kinds of people are most likely to buy this product: teenagers, parents with young children, or senior citizens (age 65 and older)?

2. Imagine that you are writing an advertisement for this product. Which three words best describe the product: *delicious, refreshing, powerful, expensive, cool*?

B SHARING INFORMATION

1 *Work in groups of four. Complete the chart with the names of products that you usually buy.*

PRODUCT	STUDENT 1	STUDENT 2	STUDENT 3	STUDENT 4
Drinks				
Snack foods				
Shampoo				
Toothpaste				

2 *Discuss these questions with your group.*

1. Do you know any TV commercials or other advertisements for these products? If so, describe the advertisements.

2. Do advertisements sometimes convince you to buy products? Explain.

C PREPARING TO READ

BACKGROUND

*How much do you know about the world of advertising? Test your knowledge. Read each statement. Write **T** (true) if you think it is true, or **F** (false) if you think it is false.*

_____ 1. To sell a product in a foreign country, a company must translate its advertisement.

_____ 2. International businesses such as McDonald's offer different products in different parts of the world.

_____ 3. When advertisers write an ad, their goal is to make people laugh.

_____ 4. Laws about advertising are basically the same all over the world.

VOCABULARY FOR COMPREHENSION

Read the words and their definitions. Then read the paragraph below that describes an imaginary new product. Complete the paragraph with the correct forms of the vocabulary words.

> **a campaign:** a planned, organized effort
> **a competition:** an activity in which people try to do better than each other;
>   **the competition:** people or things that you compete against
> **to convince:** to make someone want to do something
> **to fail:** to not do well, to not reach your goal
> **a firm:** a company, a business
> **global:** international
> **a goal:** something that people want to do
> **a market:** a group of people to whom products are sold;
>   **to market:** to try to sell a product to a certain group of people
> **a message:** information that one person gives to another
> **to succeed:** to do well, to reach your goal

Energy Plus is a group of scientists, sports players, and businesspeople. The members of this (**1**) _____*firm*_____ are working together to make a new bottled water for people who exercise regularly. People who are interested in their health are also part of the (**2**) _____ for this product. The people at Energy Plus hope to make a product that tastes delicious. Their (**3**) _____ is to finish making this product in one year. Energy Plus bottled water will be advertised on television and in magazines. All the ads in this (**4**) _____ will begin on the same date, and they will all be similar. The (**5**) _____ of the ads will be that drinking plenty of water is very important for people who exercise. A large number of people in many countries will be interested in the drink. The interest in this product will be (**6**) _____. Energy Plus will provide a special telephone number to store owners to call and get information that will (**7**) _____ them to sell Energy Plus in their stores. Several other groups are working on a similar product. Because of this (**8**) _____, the Energy Plus team plans to make the best product possible, and they hope to (**9**) _____. If they (**10**) _____, they will need to rethink their ideas and develop a better plan.

2 Focus on Reading

A READING ONE: *Advertising All over the World*

Work with a partner. Discuss problems that you think advertisers might have if they want to sell a product in different countries. List two or three problems in the space below. Share your list with the class.

Possible Problems

_____

_____

_____

Now read the following magazine article on global advertising. How many of the problems that your class discussed are mentioned in the article?

Advertising
All over the World

1   How can a rabbit be stronger than a football hero? How can a rabbit be more powerful than a big, strong man? In the world of advertising, this is quite possible. Consider the example of Jacko. This great Australian football hero recently appeared on TV and yelled at the audience to buy products. Jacko's angry campaign worked well in Australia, so Energizer® batteries invited him north to sell their product in the United States. But Jacko's yelling did not convince the American audience to buy batteries. So, good-bye, Jacko. Hello, Energizer Bunny®, the little toy rabbit that has sold far more batteries than Jacko.

2   In the world of advertising, selling products is the most important goal. As companies are becoming more global, they are looking for new ways to sell their products all over the world. It is true that because of global communication, the world is becoming smaller today.

3   But it is also true that the problems of global advertising—problems of language and culture—have become larger than ever. For example, Braniff Airlines wanted to advertise its fine leather seats. But when its advertisement was translated from English to Spanish, it told people that they could fly naked! Another example of incorrect translation is how Chevrolet tried to market the Chevy Nova in Latin America. In English, the word *nova* refers to a star. But in Spanish, it means "doesn't go." Would you buy a car with this name?

4   To avoid these problems of translation, most advertising firms are now beginning to write completely new ads. In writing new ads, global advertisers consider the different styles of communication in different countries. In some cultures, the meaning of an advertisement is usually found in the exact words that are used to describe the product and to explain why it is better than the competition. This is true in such countries as the United States, Britain, and Germany. But in other cultures, such as Japan's, the message depends more on situations and feelings than it does on words. For this reason, the goal of many TV commercials in Japan will be to show how good people feel at a party or other social situation. The commercial will not say that a product is better than others. Instead, its goal will be to create a positive mood or feeling about the product.

5   Global advertisers must also consider differences in laws and customs. For instance, certain countries will not allow TV commercials on Sunday, and others will not allow TV commercials for children's products on any day of the week. In some parts of the world, it is forbidden to show dogs on television or certain types of clothing, such as jeans. The global advertiser who does not understand such laws and customs will have problems.

6   Finally, there is the question of what to advertise. People around the world have different customs as well as different likes and dislikes. So the best advertisement in the world means nothing if the product is not right for the market. Even though some markets around the world are quite similar, companies such as McDonald's have found that it is very important to sell different products in different parts of the world. So when you go to a McDonald's in Hawaii, you'll find Chinese noodles on the menu. If you stop for a hamburger in Germany, you can order a beer with your meal. In Malaysia, you can try a milk shake that is flavored with a fruit that most people in other countries have never tasted.

7   All of these products must be sold with the right kind of message. It has never been an easy job for global advertisers to create this message. But no matter how difficult this job may be, it is very important for global advertisers to do it well. In today's competitive world, most new products quickly fail. Knowing how to advertise in the global market can help companies win the competition for success.

READING FOR MAIN IDEAS

1 *Look back at the true/false statements that you completed in Section 1C on page 2. Think about the information in Reading One. If a statement is false, rewrite it to make it true.*

write a new

Example: To sell a product in a foreign country, a company must ~~translate its~~ advertisement.

2 *Answer the questions. Then compare your answers with the class.*

1. Who is Jacko? What does he show about international advertising?

_____

_____

2. What problem do advertisers have when they try to translate ads directly from one language to another?

_____

_____

3. How can a global advertiser avoid problems?

_____

_____

4. Why should a company offer different products in different countries?

_____

_____

READING FOR DETAILS

Circle the letter of the best answer to complete the sentences below. Make sure the sentences are correct according to Reading One.

1. A battery _____ changed its campaign from Jacko to the Energizer Bunny®.
   a. company
   b. goal
   c. market
   d. translator

2. There are many problems with _____, even with languages that are similar, such as English and Spanish.
   a. advertising
   b. marketing
   c. translation
   d. competition

3. Different countries have different styles of _____, which involve different uses of words and feelings.
   a. writing
   b. communicating
   c. advertising
   d. competing

4. Some countries do not allow _____ ads for children's products.
   a. newspaper
   b. TV
   c. magazine
   d. radio

5. Drinking beer with a meal is an example of a _____.
   a. culture
   b. message
   c. custom
   d. law

6. Many new products fail because there is a lot of _____ in the world today.
   a. advertising
   b. business
   c. communication
   d. competition

7. The Chevy Nova campaign failed in Latin America because of the _____ of the ads.
   a. goal
   b. cost
   c. style
   d. message

8. Ads that show a group of people sharing good feelings are often quite successful in _____.
   a. Germany
   b. Japan
   c. Malaysia
   d. Britain

REACTING TO THE READING

1 *Think about what you learned in Reading One, and circle the best answer to complete the sentences. On the left, note which paragraph in the reading the answer came from.*

_6_ 1. A Baskin Robbins ice cream commercial in the Philippines might advertise mango and papaya ice cream as a new flavor because _____.
   a. Baskin Robbins is introducing this flavor globally
   b. Filipinos love mango and papaya
   c. this product was successful in the United States

____ 2. A shampoo commercial shows a young woman running in slow motion toward her handsome boyfriend. Her long, thick, shiny hair bounces up and down while romantic music plays in the background. As she runs into the arms of her boyfriend, he twirls her around, and we see her beautiful, smiling face. This picture is replaced by a picture of the shampoo. There is no written or spoken language of any kind. This commercial is probably from _____.
   a. Britain
   b. Australia
   c. Japan

____ 3. A luxury car commercial shows the car driving on a curvy road through beautiful green hills. Classical music plays in the background as the narrator explains why this car is better than all other cars. This commercial is probably from _____.
   a. the United States
   b. Latin America
   c. Japan

____ 4. Most likely, _____ caused the Jacko advertising campaign to fail in the United States.
   a. differences in product preferences
   b. differences in customs
   c. problems in translation

____ 5. A few years ago, the U.S. drugstore chain Sav-on was renamed Osco because that was the name of the company's new owner. This created serious problems, however, because *osco* sounds like a Spanish word that means "repulsive." Spanish-speaking customers didn't like the name, so it was changed back to Sav-on. This is an example of _____.
   a. differences in product preferences
   b. differences in customs
   c. problems in translation

2 *Discuss the following questions with your classmates.*

1. Think of a popular food or drink product from your home country (for example, tamales, green tea, sea cucumbers, or frozen TV dinners). Where else in the world do you think the product would do well? Where wouldn't it do well?

2. In your home country, is the meaning of an advertisement more likely to be found in the exact words used to describe the product or in the feeling and mood the advertisement creates? Give an example from your country that illustrates your answer.

B   READING TWO: *Changing World Markets*

Read the following speech. Julia Ross, the president of the Global Advertisers' Association, recently spoke at a meeting of advertisers who want to start global campaigns. Part of her speech was published in Adworld *magazine. Discuss the following questions with the class before you read.*

1. Do you know of any countries in which the government doesn't allow businesses to advertise? Which countries? Why do you think the government doesn't allow businesses to advertise in these countries?

2. Do you know anyone who has lived in a country where it is difficult for people to buy the products they want? If yes, why is it difficult to buy the products they want? When they want something very badly, what do they do?

CHANGING WORLD MARKETS

By Julia Ross (from *Adworld*)

1   Good morning. It's good to be here with you all. My goal today is to give you some information about changing world markets. Let's start by looking at the U.S.A. Can you think of a country with more advertising than the United States? Think about watching a movie on TV. You're waiting for the good guy to get the bad guy, and suddenly there's a commercial. A few minutes later the good guy is in trouble, and you're interrupted by another commercial. Message after message. It's not like that in other countries. In places like France and Spain, you can watch at least a half hour of the program before a commercial interruption. And then the commercials will come all in a row.

2   China is a different story. For years any kind of commercial advertising was illegal.

Government advertising was all over the place, but business advertising was nonexistent. Then Sony came along and changed things. The Japanese companies were the first to start advertising in China. They've led the way for others to come into the country. We can learn something from them, too. It's important not to come in overnight and start advertising because that can lead to serious mistakes. Advertisers must take their time and plan their campaigns carefully. Because there are millions of people in China who don't know what a Big Mac is, you wouldn't want to rush over there and try to sell them one. Instead, you would want to plan ahead five or ten years. It pays to be patient in China.

3   Now in Russia, you would have to think about your product and whether or not there's a market for it. Fast food, for example, is a very strange idea in Russia. In their restaurants, you sit down and the waiter brings you soup, salad, meat, and potatoes— one thing at a time. The Russians think of food as something you take your time with, something you enjoy.

4   What happened with pizza in Russia is a very funny story. First they had to convince people to try it, and they had to explain that it was similar to Russian *vatrushka*. Then the Pizzeria restaurant opened up in Moscow. The Russians may have liked it all right, but Pizzeria didn't go over too well with foreign visitors because the pizza didn't always have enough tomato sauce and cheese! Another problem was that if you wanted to take the pizza home with you, the chef wouldn't hear of it. He didn't want it to get cold. When you're dealing with international markets, you're dealing with other customs, other cultures.

5   But things are changing every day. New markets are opening up all the time. We have to look at the big picture before we start planning a campaign. We need to think about our product. Will people be able to buy it? Regarding our marketing plan, will people understand it? Remember that for years in China and Russia, people had a hard time buying things. The best advertisement of all was a long line in front of a store. That's how people knew which store was the place to go. So we must think about how things are changing if we expect to be successful. I appreciate your attendance today. It's been a pleasure to be with you.

C   LINKING READINGS ONE AND TWO

1   *Imagine that you are an advertiser who read Julia Ross's speech in* Adworld. *What did you learn? How is this information related to the problems of global advertising described in Reading One? Consider such areas as laws, customs, and likes/dislikes. Complete the following letter with your own ideas.*

Dear Ms. Ross:

I recently read part of your speech in *Adworld*. I was especially interested to learn that _____

_____ .

It was also interesting to hear that _____

_____ .

I have a few questions for you. _____

_____

_____

_____

_____

Thank you for taking the time to respond to my letter.

Sincerely,

_____

2 *Work with a partner. Compare advertising in your home country to advertising in another country. Use the following questions for your discussion. Then share your ideas with the class.*

- How do advertisers convince people to buy products?

- Are there any laws that advertisers must follow? What are they?

- What kinds of problems do you think advertisers have when they translate ads from other cultures into the language of your home culture?

3 Focus on Vocabulary

1 *Read each sentence and the four words or phrases that follow. Three of the answer choices are synonyms (words that have similar meaning) for the underlined word. Cross out the word or phrase that is NOT a synonym.*

1. The <u>goal</u> of the advertising campaign was to sell more cars to women.
   - **a.** purpose
   - **b.** plan
   - **c.** hope
   - **d.** ~~future~~

2. Women with young children are part of a growing <u>market</u>.
   - **a.** group of people
   - **b.** group of stores
   - **c.** group of buyers
   - **d.** group of customers

3. The ad's <u>message</u> was that the new cars were safe.
   - **a.** idea
   - **b.** information
   - **c.** style
   - **d.** story

4. The ads were <u>successful</u> because many women believed in the safety of the cars.
   - **a.** effective
   - **b.** certain
   - **c.** satisfactory
   - **d.** convincing

5. As a result, the ads <u>convinced</u> mothers to buy the cars.
   - **a.** encouraged
   - **b.** pushed
   - **c.** persuaded
   - **d.** forced

6. However, the ads <u>failed to sell</u> cars to single women without children.
   - **a.** didn't sell
   - **b.** couldn't sell
   - **c.** were unable to sell
   - **d.** tried to sell

7. The advertising campaign will become <u>global</u> next year.
   - **a.** multinational
   - **b.** worldwide
   - **c.** organized
   - **d.** international

8. Ads for <u>the competition</u> will not become global.
   - **a.** race
   - **b.** other companies
   - **c.** other sellers
   - **d.** different firms

2 *Idioms* *are phrases that have a special meaning. The meaning of the phrase is very different from the meanings of the separate words. Idioms are often used in conversation. The sentences below are from Reading Two. Match the underlined idiom in each sentence with its definition below.*

_____ 1. In places like France and Spain, you can watch at least a half hour of the program before a commercial interruption. And then the commercials come <u>all in a row</u>.

_____ 2. Government advertising was <u>all over the place</u>, but business advertising was nonexistent.

_____ 3. It's important not to <u>come in overnight</u> and start advertising because that can lead to serious mistakes.

_____ 4. Advertisers must <u>take their time</u> and plan their campaigns carefully.

_____ 5. The Russians may have liked it all right, but Pizzeria <u>didn't go over too well</u> with foreign visitors because the pizza didn't always have enough tomato sauce and cheese!

_____ 6. Another problem was that if you wanted to take the pizza home with you, the chef <u>wouldn't hear of it</u>. He didn't want it to get cold.

_____ 7. New markets are opening up all the time. We have to <u>look at the big picture</u> before we start planning a campaign. We need to think about our product.

_____ 8. Remember that for years in China and Russia, people <u>had a hard time</u> buying things.

a. said "no" strongly	**e.** very common
b. had difficulty	**f.** enter quickly
c. one after another	**g.** be careful
d. did not succeed	**h.** consider the general situation

3 *Work in groups of three. Write a commercial using at least five new words or idioms from Exercises 1 and 2. Your commercial can be serious or funny. It can be a narration or a conversation advertising cars, clothing, computers, airlines, snacks, dating services, or diets. After you have written it, your teacher will check your grammar. Then read or act out your commercial for your classmates.*

You can begin your commercial with one of these lines:

"Hello. I'm _____ and I've got good news for you."
"The new _____ is everything you always wanted in a car."
"Are you tired? bored? Do you need a change? Well, . . ."

You can end your commercial with one of these lines:

"To find out more, call . . . Get yours today!"
"Call now for more information or log on to . . ."
"Feel the difference."

4 Focus on Writing

A STYLE: Paragraph Development

1 *Read the following paragraph from "Advertising All over the World." Then discuss the questions with the class.*

Global advertisers must also consider differences in laws and customs. For instance, certain countries will not allow TV commercials on Sunday, and others will not allow TV commercials for children's products on any day of the week. In some parts of the world, it is forbidden to show dogs on television or certain types of clothing, such as jeans. The global advertiser who does not understand such laws and customs will have problems.

1. Where is the main idea? Circle it.

2. Where are the examples? Underline them.

3. How many examples are there?

A paragraph usually presents one **main idea.** The sentence that states the main idea is called a **topic sentence.** The topic sentence is often the first sentence of the paragraph. The following sentences support the topic sentence with examples and details. The **concluding sentence** at the end of the paragraph repeats key words from the topic sentence. Look at the following examples:

Topic Sentence: Global advertisers must consider differences in laws and customs.

- **Example 1:** Some countries do not allow TV advertisements on Sunday.

- **Example 2:** Other countries never allow TV advertisements for children's products.

- **Example 3:** In some parts of the world, dogs and jeans cannot be shown on television.

Concluding Sentence: The global advertiser who does not understand such laws and customs will have problems.

2 *Identify each sentence below as follows:*

TS = Topic Sentence   **D1** = Detail 1   **D3** = Detail 3
CS = Concluding Sentence   **D2** = Detail 2

_____ 1. The commercials give the same message in different languages: "Time with family is priceless."

_____ 2. It is trying to appeal to a new market: the everyday person who values family.

_____ 3. MasterCard knows that family values have an international appeal because it has done market research and proved it.

_____ 4. MasterCard is changing its advertising campaign for the global market.

_____ 5. As a result, this campaign is working successfully around the world.

3 *Now write the paragraph on a separate piece of paper by putting the sentences in the correct order. Indent the first sentence.*

B   GRAMMAR: Contrast—Simple Present and Present Progressive

1 *Compare the following sentences from Reading Two. Notice the phrases or words that are bold. How are they different?*

You're waiting for the good guy to get the bad guy, and suddenly there's a commercial.

The Russians **think** of food as something you take your time with, something you **enjoy.**

But things **are changing** every day.

Simple Present and Present Progressive

1. The simple present tense is used to describe what sometimes happens, what usually happens, or what always happens.	The commercials **give** the same message in different languages: "Time with family is priceless."
2. We often use the simple present tense with adverbs of frequency to express how often something happens: *always, usually, often, sometimes, rarely/seldom, never.*	In some cultures, the meaning of an advertisement **is usually** found in the exact words that are used to describe the product and to explain why it is better than the competition.

(continued)

3. Non-action verbs describe emotions, mental states, and situations.

I **appreciate** your attendance today. (emotion)

MasterCard **knows** that family values have an international appeal because it has done market research and proved it. (mental state)

Fast food, for example, **is** a very strange idea in Russia. (situation)

4. The present progressive tense is used to describe actions that are happening at the present time.

MasterCard **is changing** its advertising campaign for the global market.

This campaign **is working** successfully around the world.

5. We often use words or phrases such as *today, nowadays, this month, these days, this year* with the present progressive.

Because of global communication, the world **is becoming** smaller **today.**

2 *Read the following sentences. Complete each one with the correct verb tense.*

1. Many people _____ that there is nothing wrong with eating
(believe / are believing)
fast food once in a while.

2. The number of fast-food restaurants around the world _____.
(increases / is increasing)

3. These restaurants usually _____ different foods in different
(serve / are serving)
parts of the world.

4. Many people _____ McDonald's to be an excellent example
(consider / are considering)
of a successful global restaurant.

5. Now, advertising firms _____ different ads for different
(write / are writing)
countries because of the various styles of communication.

6. Television ads for fast food always _____ the food look
(make / are making)
delicious.

3 *Complete the sentences below with your own ideas. Use the simple present and present progressive.*

1. These days, famous people who appear in advertisements _____ _____ .

2. When a TV commercial begins, some people _____ .

3. Now, TV commercials _____ .

C   WRITING TOPICS

Write a paragraph about one of the following topics. Use some of the vocabulary, grammar, and style that you learned in this unit.

1. Describe a commercial that you enjoy watching on TV. What is its message? How does it convince people to buy the product?

2. Some countries have laws that forbid advertising campaigns for tobacco and alcohol on TV. Do you agree or disagree with these laws? Explain your opinion, and support it with reasons.

3. Describe a time when an advertisement convinced you to buy something. Were you satisfied with the product? Give details about your experience.

D   RESEARCH TOPIC

A billboard is a large outdoor board used for advertisements. Look at billboard advertisements in your community.

Choose one billboard, and complete the following worksheet.

Step 1: Name of product: _____

Type of product: _____

Message (pictures, words, or both): _____

_____

Possible markets: _____

_____

Will the ad be successful locally?   Yes   No   Maybe

Explanation: _____

_____

_____

Step 2: Work in small groups to combine all your information on the chart.

	MESSAGE	MARKET	WILL THE AD SUCCEED locally?	globally?
Product 1 _____				
Product 2 _____				
Product 3 _____				
Product 4 _____				

Step 3: Discuss whether these same ads would be successful globally. If not, how would they have to be changed to succeed? Add this information to your chart.

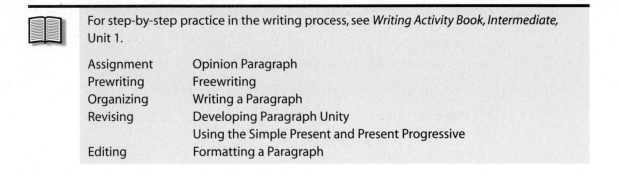

For step-by-step practice in the writing process, see *Writing Activity Book, Intermediate,* Unit 1.

Assignment	Opinion Paragraph
Prewriting	Freewriting
Organizing	Writing a Paragraph
Revising	Developing Paragraph Unity
	Using the Simple Present and Present Progressive
Editing	Formatting a Paragraph

For Unit 1 Internet activities, visit the NorthStar Companion Website at http://www.longman.com/northstar.

Going to Extremes: Sports and Obsession

1 Focus on the Topic

A PREDICTING

Look at the photograph, and discuss these questions with the class.

1. What is the man in the photo doing? How does he feel about his sport?

2. What kind of person participates in this sport?

3. Read the title of this unit. What do you think it means?

B   SHARING INFORMATION

People who are excellent at sports usually have to practice very hard. They spend many hours a week trying to improve their sports ability. Sometimes the sports that they play are dangerous.

1 *Complete the chart below about yourself. Then ask three other classmates, and write their answers.*

	YOU	CLASSMATE 1	CLASSMATE 2	CLASSMATE 3
1. Which sports do you play?				
2. How often do you practice your sport?				
3. Would you like to practice more? Why or why not?				
4. How dangerous is your sport?				

2 *Now discuss these questions with the class.*

1. Who spends the most time practicing a sport?

2. Who plays the most dangerous sport?

C   PREPARING TO READ

BACKGROUND

An **obsession** is a very strong desire to do or be something. For example, many famous athletes have obsessions. They might practice for very long hours, which could have a positive result when they win an Olympic gold medal. Their obsessions could also mean that they do something dangerous.

Work with a partner to match the name of the famous athlete to the obsession. Write the letter of the obsession next to the name. Then discuss your answers with the class.

_____ **1.** Muhammad Ali (boxer)

_____ **2.** Nadia Comaneci (gymnast)

_____ **3.** Evel Knievel (motorcyclist)

_____ **4.** Arnold Schwarzenegger (bodybuilder)

a. jumping across the Grand Canyon

b. having the most well-developed body in the world

c. wanting to be "The Greatest"

d. winning as many medals as possible

VOCABULARY FOR COMPREHENSION

Circle the definition that best matches the meaning of each underlined word.

1. This was my sister's first time skiing, so it was hard for her to <u>make it</u> down the mountain.

    a. create something

    b. finish doing something

2. The girl's classmates thought that she was a <u>freak</u> because she was interested in nothing but snowboarding.

    a. person who is in danger

    b. person who is strange or unusual

3. Playing golf on weekends is a relaxing <u>escape</u> for the busy doctor.

    a. a way to forget about problems

    b. an exciting adventure

4. The bodybuilder stopped training because of <u>intense</u> pain in his shoulders.

    a. very strong

    b. minor

5. If you <u>get hooked on</u> tennis, you will want to play it every day.

    a. get hurt while playing

    b. become unable to stop doing something

6. He was a <u>decent</u> gymnast, but he was not good enough to go to the Olympics.

    a. excellent

    b. average

7. Everyone clapped and cheered because of the <u>awesome</u> motorcycle trick.

    a. amazing

    b. simple

8. There is a <u>controversy</u> about skateboarding in public places because of its danger.

    a. public law

    b. strong disagreement

9. One of the <u>benefits</u> of running is that it makes your heart stronger.

    a. rewards

    b. goals

10. The team practices hard to <u>accomplish</u> the goal of winning a championship.

    a. make an effort

    b. succeed in doing something

2 Focus on Reading

A   READING ONE: *An Interview with Tony Hawk*

You are going to read an imaginary interview with Tony Hawk, a professional skateboarder. Before you read, write down three questions that you think the interviewer will ask Mr. Hawk about his sport and his life.

1. _____

2. _____

3. _____

Interview with Tony Hawk

from *Wheels on Fire* magazine

Tony Hawk, 1999 Summer X Games, San Francisco

Wheels on Fire (WOF): Let's start with the high point of your career. Can you pick one out to share with us?

Tony Hawk (TH): Oh yes, definitely. For me, the high point came when I was traveling to France and I had to fill out a tourist information card. You know, the thing you fill out when you're entering a new country? Well, I got to write down "skateboarder" as my occupation. How cool!

WOF: You mean that was better than what you accomplished at the 1999 Summer X Games?

TH: You mean landing the 900[1]? That was awesome, too. But that was pure obsession—story of my life. Nothing new for me there.

WOF: How was landing that trick an obsession for you?

TH: Well, like everything else I do on a skateboard, I have to get it right. It took me 13 years of practice to perfect the 900, and on that day, I think it took me something like 12 times before I made it.

WOF: Did you really work on one trick for 13 years? That does seem like an obsession!

TH: Yeah, but you know, it's a good obsession—if you can say that obsession is good. It's like this—I was this weird, skinny kid at school. Once I got into skateboarding

---

[1] *900:* a very difficult trick where you rotate two and a half times

and started wearing baggy skater clothes, it got worse. I was a freak. All the jocks[2] picked on me. And I didn't have a chance with the girls—forget it. But skating—that was my escape. Every day after school I escaped to the skate park, and the focus on skating, this really intense focus that took all my concentration—I guess that was one way I could block out all the pain of growing up.

WOF: Did your parents support your obsession with skating?

TH: Yeah, they were great. Mom took me and some friends down to the Oasis Skate Park when we were about 10 years old. They had this flat beginners' area where you could practice before you were ready to skate in the empty swimming pools. I was so skinny that the skate equipment didn't even fit me right. But once I got hooked, nothing else mattered. I drew pictures of skating all day, and I even skated in the house.

WOF: Your parents let you skate in the house?

TH: Yeah. They were pretty cool. Mom and Dad were older when they had me, so I guess you can say they were relaxed enough to let me do what I needed to do.

WOF: How about your schoolwork? Were you able to get by in school?

TH: Yeah, that was fine. I don't mean to brag or anything, but I was a gifted student. So I was able to get my schoolwork done with decent grades. My only problem was being able to sit still in class. I had so much physical energy. But school was basically OK for me until some of the teachers started taking my skateboard away. They started lecturing me about the dangers of the sport.

WOF: That couldn't stop you from skating!

TH: No way. The cool thing was that my parents worked it out for me to go to a different high school. The principal there was awesome. He let us design our own PE [physical education] classes, so take a wild guess. What class did I create?

WOF: Skateboarding.

TH: You got it. That was my PE class. By that time, I was turning professional and starting to win prize money at competitions. During summer vacation, I was able to travel around to cool places like Australia, Europe, and Canada. I was able to show off some techniques.

WOF: Is that when your new style became famous?

TH: Yeah. You know, a lot of other skaters had this smooth, flowing style. Compared to them, I was kind of like a robot. And I was always coming up with new tricks, new surprises.

WOF: When did they first call you the Michael Jordan of skateboarding?

TH: I guess that was back in '95 at the Extreme Games. You remember—that event they had on the sports channel? That was a combination of skateboarding, BMX cycling, and rollerblading. There were a lot of good skaters there. I was just the one who got the attention. That's how TV is—I guess they can only focus on one thing at a time. But there were a lot of outstanding people there, believe me.

WOF: Let's go back to the high point. Now that you've looked back on your career a bit, was it still being able to write "skateboarder" as your occupation?

TH: Yeah. I love that. You know, there's so much controversy about skateboarding—some people think it's a crime and they don't want us to skate in public places, but I just love being able to say it's my occupation. My occupation and my obsession!

WOF: As an occupation, it has rewarded you pretty well, wouldn't you say?

TH: Yeah, there were some great benefits along the way—like being able to buy my

---

[2] *jocks:* slang term meaning "athletes"

own home when I was still in high school. And later, being able to buy another home out in the desert—and build my own skate park. But now that I think about it, you know what I'm really proud of accomplishing?

WOF: Making skateboard history when you landed the 900?

TH: Nope. It was having Disney animators use some of my tricks in the Tarzan movie. When my son watched Tarzan swinging through the trees, he realized that it had something to do with me. And he thought I was awesome! Now that's the greatest feeling you can get, believe me.

READING FOR MAIN IDEAS

*Write **T** (true) or **F** (false) for each statement.*

_____   1. Tony Hawk is ashamed of his occupation.

_____   2. He wants all his skateboard tricks to be perfect.

_____   3. His classmates liked him because of his skateboarding ability.

_____   4. His parents thought that skateboarding was a waste of time.

_____   5. He had a smooth and flowing style.

_____   6. He earned a lot of money before the age of 25.

READING FOR DETAILS

Write one-sentence answers to the questions. Then compare answers with a partner.

1. What did Tony Hawk accomplish at the 1999 Summer X Games?

_____

2. How much time did he spend practicing his most famous trick?

_____

3. When did he begin skateboarding?

_____

4. Where did he learn to ride a skateboard?

_____

5. What kind of problems did he have in school?

_____

6. Who saw Tony's tricks in a Tarzan movie?

_____

REACTING TO THE READING

1 *Read the following imaginary conversation between Tony Hawk's parents at the Summer X Games in San Francisco. Work with a partner to complete the conversation. Use information from Reading One.*

MOM: I hope Tony can land the 900 today.

DAD: Me, too. He's been practicing that trick for years!

MOM: I know. That's our boy. He's only happy when _____.

DAD: True. He wants to be the best. Do you remember how he
          _____ after school?

MOM: Yes! Looking back now, I guess that helped him because
          _____.

DAD: You're right. Hey—look at him now! He's going to make it!

MOM: Go, Tony! Go! Look at that. I'm so proud of him.

DAD: That's our Tony—a real _____.

2 *Work in small groups. Discuss the good and bad points of being a young athlete like Tony Hawk. List them below. Then share your ideas with the class.*

GOOD POINTS	BAD POINTS
You learn to be very disciplined.	It takes time away from schoolwork.

3 Tony Hawk said that his obsession with skateboarding helped him to block some of the pain of growing up. What do you think he means? In your opinion, is this a good point or a bad point? Explain your answer in the space below. Then share your ideas with a classmate.

_____

_____

_____

_____

_____

B | **READING TWO:** *High School Star Hospitalized for Eating Disorder*

1 Read the following newspaper article about a high school gymnast.

High School Star Hospitalized for Eating Disorder

1 Sierra High School gymnast Ashley Lindermann was hospitalized Tuesday for complications related to anorexia nervosa. Her coach, Dianne Coyle, says that she will not be returning to the gymnastics team this season.

2 "It's really a loss—not only to the team but also to Ashley personally," says Coyle. "She had hopes of qualifying for the Olympics. But her health comes first, of course. Once she is better, I'm sure she can get back into the sport and go for the gold."

3 Dr. Paula Kim, director of the Eating Disorders Clinic at Baldwin Hospital, explains that it is not unusual for athletes, especially gymnasts, to become obsessed with their weight. One reason for this is that in gymnastics, the lighter the body, the more skillfully it can perform. She explains that an obsession with weight can lead to extreme dieting, which affects not only the body but also the mind.

4 "For the anorexic, the mental focus becomes very small: food and weight. In a way, it's easy to see how this helps the anorexic manage the fear of living in the big, uncontrollable world out there. You may not be able to control how other people feel about you, but you can control what you put in your mouth. You can also control how many hours you spend at the gym. Soon you get hooked on controlling your weight."

5   High school counselor Lisa Rodriguez has expressed concern that Lindermann's illness is related to pressure.

6   "There's an enormous amount of pressure that goes along with training for the Olympics," she says. "I know that she comes from an athletic family—I think that's why she felt she had to accomplish so much in sports. Also, when you talk about the Olympics, you're talking about being the best of the best. I think that added to Ashley's feeling of pressure."

7   Since joining the Sierra High gymnastics team as a sophomore two years ago, Ashley has broken all school records and led the team to three regional championships.

8   Coach Coyle says, "As soon as I met Ashley, I could tell right away that she was obsessed with the sport. And that's not the kind of athlete that you have to push. My goal with Ashley was to try and help her have more of a balanced life. I talked to her about how she was doing in her classes, what she might want to study in college. I also told her and all the members on the team to take at least one or two days a week just to let their bodies rest. I know there's some controversy about her situation, but all I can say is that I'm very, very sorry that Ashley got sick."

9   Coyle's concern for Lindermann's health is shared by her teammates and friends. Some of them recall how the tiny gymnastics star worked out at the health club in addition to hours of regular practice with the team. They describe how the walls of her bedroom are covered with photos of Olympic winners—Mary Lou Retton and Nadia Comaneci to name a few.

10   Lindermann, who currently weighs only 72 pounds (32.6 kgs.), is expected to remain in the hospital for at least a few months.

2 *Circle the best answer to complete the statements below.*

1. Ashley's coach hopes that she will leave the hospital and _____.
   a. focus on her health
   b. join the Olympic team

2. Anorexia nervosa is an obsession with _____.
   a. exercise
   b. weight

3. One reason for becoming anorexic is that it gives you a feeling of _____.
   a. more control
   b. mental focus

4. Some of the pressure in Ashley's life was because she wanted to be the best gymnast in her _____.
   a. high school
   b. country

5. Before she went to the hospital, her coach had been pushing her to focus on gymnastics _____.
   a. less
   b. more

C LINKING READINGS ONE AND TWO

1 *Work in small groups. Discuss the following questions. Then share your ideas with the class.*

   a. How are Tony Hawk and Ashley Lindermann similar? How are they different?

   b. Which athlete do you think is more obsessed with sports?

   c. Why do more gymnasts than skateboarders become anorexic? Explain.

2 *Sometimes an obsession with sports can help an athlete to practice harder and improve. But for some people, an obsession with sports can lead to physical or mental health problems. Look at the list of reasons why people can develop an obsession with sports. Write **T** (Tony) and/or **A** (Ashley) next to the reasons that you think influenced them. Then discuss your answers with a partner.*

Reasons for developing an obsession with sports:

_____ family pressure   _____ peer pressure

_____ desire to be the best   _____ (other reason) _____

_____ childhood experiences

3 Focus on Vocabulary

1 *Complete the chart below by adding different forms of each word. Use a dictionary to look up any words that you don't know. An **X** indicates there is no form in that category.*

Noun	Verb	Adjective	Adverb
1.	accomplish		X
2. escape			X
3.	X	controversial	
4. benefit			
5.			obsessively
6.		intense	
7. perfection			
8.		practiced	X

2 *Read the following paragraph about Gelsey Kirkland, author of* Dancing on My Grave. *Complete the paragraph with the vocabulary words in their correct form.*

benefit	obsessed	obsessive	obsession
awesome	escape	hooked on	intense

Gelsey Kirkland was a professional ballerina with the New York City Ballet and the American Ballet Theater. She became (**1**) _____ with having a thin body. As a result of her (**2**) _____, she ate a very small amount of food. For example, she sometimes ate only one apple a day while following a very (**3**) _____ dance practice schedule. Her feelings toward Mikhail Barishnikov, who was considered one of the most

(**4**) "_____" male dancers in the world, also became (**5**) _____. Sadly, her love for Barishnikov caused her much personal pain, and to (**6**) _____ from her unhappiness, she began using drugs and got (**7**) _____ them. Finally, she wrote a book about her life and career entitled *Dancing on My Grave*. Perhaps readers of this book will (**8**) _____ from learning about the experience of this talented, yet unhappy, dancer.

3 *In this unit, you have read about the accomplishments of some famous people. Now think about the accomplishments in your life. You may consider different areas of life: sports, school, work, hobbies, or family.*
   On a separate piece of paper, write a paragraph describing one of your most important accomplishments. Use at least four of the following words in your paragraph.

hooked on	intense	obsession	escape	benefit	accomplish

4 Focus on Writing

1 *A news article is one example of a factual report. Look back at the newspaper article in Reading Two. How is it different from the style of Reading One? What do you think is the purpose of the newspaper article?*

> Good newspaper articles answer five basic questions—called the 5Ws. Important information includes:
>
> **Who** is the story about?
> **What** is the story about?
> **When** did the story take place?
> **Where** did the story take place?
> **Why** or **How** did the story happen?
>
> In a factual report, quotations (people's exact words) may also be used to give more facts or opinions.

2 *Now go back to Reading Two, and look for the answers to the 5Ws. Underline important information in the text, and write the question words in the margin.*

Example

who
when, what

Sierra High School gymnast Ashley Lindermann was hospitalized Tuesday for complications related to anorexia nervosa. Her coach, Dianne Coyle, says that she will not be returning to the gymnastics team this season.

3 *Now use the underlined information to write a short paragraph with the important facts from the article. Share your paragraph with a classmate.*

4 *Read the information below about a new educational video produced by Kristy Pham, a student at Sierra High. Label each fact with one of the 5Ws. Then use the information to write a factual report about the video.*

_____ Fact #1: Kristy Pham is the captain of the Sierra High gymnastics team.

_____ Fact #2: The video was produced last week in the Sierra High TV production class.

_____ Fact #3: The video will be shown next weekend at the Sierra Bonita Public Library.

_____ Fact #4: The purpose of the video is to educate the public about the dangers of anorexia nervosa.

_____ Fact #5: The video will include an interview with Ashley Lindermann's teammates and coach.

B   GRAMMAR: Modals of Ability

1 _Look at the following examples from Reading One. Think about the meaning of the underlined words._

I guess that was one way I <u>could</u> block out all the pain of growing up.

They had this flat beginners' area where you <u>could</u> practice before you were ready to skate in the empty swimming pools.

<u>Were you able</u> to get by in school?

Mom and Dad were older when they had me, so I guess you <u>can</u> say they were relaxed enough to let me do what I needed to do.

Modals and Related Verbs That Show Ability

1. To describe ability in the present, use **_can._**	He **can** do skateboard tricks.
2. To describe ability in the present or future, use **_be able to._**	She **is able to** swim fast. (present)
	He**'s not able to** ride a horse. (negative present)
	They **will be able to** win the race. (future)
	(continued)

3. To describe general ability in the past, use *could* or *was/were able to.*

When he was a boy, he **could** ride his bike all day.

Last winter, they **were able to** ski four times.

He **wasn't able to** join the Olympic team. (past negative)

4. The modals *can* and *could* have only one form. To describe ability in forms other than present tense (*can*) or past tense (*could*), it is necessary to use *be able to.*

She wants **to be able to** run faster. (verb + infinitive)

They have **been able to** win two championships. (present perfect)

2 *A young skateboarder wrote a letter to Tony Hawk. Complete the sentences with verbs of ability. Use* **can, can't, could, couldn't,** *or* **be able to.**

Dear Mr. Hawk,

My name is Michael Craig, and I live in Florida. I am nine years old, and I guess you (**1**) _____ say that I'm obsessed with skateboarding. My dream is to (**2**) _____ ride a skateboard like you do. I (**3**) _____ believe your tricks! Last week I started practicing the 900, but I (**4**) _____ make it. My mom came outside and started yelling at me. She thought I (**5**) _____ kill myself doing that trick, but I told her not to worry.

I'm a pretty decent skateboarder for my age. How old were you when you (**6**) _____ finally land a 900? I want to (**7**) _____ do that by my tenth birthday. I'm going to practice a lot.

Mr. Hawk, I know that you're a busy professional skateboarder, but I really hope that you will (**8**) _____ write me back soon. (**9**) _____ you please find time for a skateboarding star of the future?

Thanks for reading my letter. Keep up the intense skateboarding. You're the best!

Yours truly,

Michael Craig

C WRITING TOPICS

Choose one of the following topics. Write two or three paragraphs using some of the vocabulary, grammar, and style that you learned in this unit.

1. Who is a famous athlete that you admire? What has he or she accomplished? Write a factual report about this famous athlete.

2. Some activities other than sports can lead to a dangerous obsession. For example, some people enjoy watching their favorite movie stars so much that they begin stalking, or obsessively following, the stars. Other examples include shopping and using the Internet. Explain how obsession with an activity can become dangerous.

3. Some sports such as skydiving or skateboarding can injure or even kill people. As a result, there is controversy about whether or not such sports should be legal in public areas. Give your opinion.

4. The pressure to do well in an activity such as ballet or gymnastics is one reason why people develop anorexia nervosa and other eating disorders. Describe a few more reasons why some people have serious problems with their bodies, weight, and food. Consider how family pressure and media images are related to this issue.

D RESEARCH TOPIC

Step 1: Find a person (or team) in your community who has had significant accomplishments in sports or dance. Interview the person or team leader. You may also gather information about the person or team by reading local newspaper articles and/or Websites.

Step 2: Use the information to write a factual report about this person's life and accomplishments. Refer to the following questions in writing your report.

- WHO is this person or team? What kind of early life and education did he or she have? Who are other important people related to this person or team?

- WHAT are the greatest accomplishments of this person or team? What kind of problems have been faced?

- WHEN did this person or team become well known? When and where did this person's accomplishments take place?

- WHERE did this person or team first become involved in dance or sports? Where has this person or team traveled?

- WHY has this person or team become so successful? How much practice and training has been involved? Has obsession helped them in any way?

Step 3:   Read your report to a small group of classmates. Work together to choose the most interesting report to share with the class.

For step-by-step practice in the writing process, see *Writing Activity Book, Intermediate,* Unit 2.

Assignment	Descriptive Paragraph
Prewriting	Interviewing
Organizing	Using Time Order
Revising	Considering Your Audience
	Using Modals of Ability
Editing	Rules for Capitalization

For Unit 2 Internet activities, visit the NorthStar Companion Website at http://www.longman.com/northstar.

Miracle Cure?

Lose the Fat Around Your Waist and on Your Belly Now

Lose up to 5 inches in only 50 days!

Get that sculptured, hard look that women love.

Use Sculptured Body and lose up to 5 inches from your belly in 50 days or less—without even exercising!

Sculptured Body contains only organic ingredients that help you lose fat. Available to you by calling 1-800-555-5555.

Sculptured Body guarantees you will have the body women love, or your money back.

1 Focus on the Topic

A PREDICTING

Look at the advertisement, and discuss these questions with the class.

1. What does the product in the ad promise to do?

2. Do you think it works? Why or why not?

B SHARING INFORMATION

*A **treatment** is a way to cure a sickness or to improve a person's health. Below is a chart with several different treatments. Add a treatment you've tried. Interview a partner about the treatments. Check (✓) the appropriate columns. Discuss your results with the class.*

Treatment	Partner has seen ads on TV or in magazines	Partner has used it or knows someone who has used it	It worked	It didn't work
1. Your treatment: _____				
2. An herb tea to cure a cold				
3. A drink for quick weight loss				
4. A cream to grow hair				
5. A cream to remove wrinkles				
6. An animal product to cure cancer				

C PREPARING TO READ

BACKGROUND

Read the statements below, and answer the questions that follow.

Facts about Quackery*

- Americans spend $27 billion a year getting their medical treatment from quacks.**

- 38 million Americans have used a quack's products or treatments in the past year.

---

* *quackery:* the practice of pretending to have medical knowledge or pretending to be able to cure diseases or stop the effects of aging
** *quacks:* people who sell health products or treatments that don't work

- One out of ten people who uses a quack's products is hurt in some way.

- 60% of the people hurt by quacks are elderly.

- A telephone survey by the American Cancer Society found that 9 percent of American cancer patients had used quack treatments.

- A survey of 166 doctors found that 25 cancer patient deaths may have been caused by a quack treatment.

- It is possible that more than $1 billion per year is spent on quack treatments (the same amount used for cancer research each year).

1. Some people don't go to a doctor when they are sick. They go to a person who gives them a treatment they believe will help them. Why do many people want to avoid going to a doctor?

2. From the facts above, we learn that quacks sell more than half of their products to elderly people. Why do you think the elderly buy these products?

VOCABULARY FOR COMPREHENSION

Circle the letter of the best definition for the underlined word(s) in each sentence.

1. Hi, my name is Anne. I'm depressed because I recently lost a lot of money. I was the underline victim of a quack. A victim is _____.
   a. a person who is hurt by someone or something else
   b. a person who is helped by someone or something else
   c. a person who wants to help someone or something else

2. Here's what happened. I wanted to get a job as a flight attendant on an airplane. The problem is that I had to lose ten pounds within one week to be able to get the job. It seemed impossible. Then I saw an ad in the newspaper for a quick weight-loss product. The ad said I could lose fourteen pounds in one week! It seemed like a miracle because I could lose the ten pounds and get the job. A miracle is _____.
   a. a normal event
   b. a surprising and wonderful event
   c. an impossible event

3. The quick weight-loss product was a drink. The drink was the discovery of a man who went to the Amazon forest. Some tribal people living in the forest taught him how to make the drink. They had been making this drink for hundreds of years. A discovery involves _____.
   a. finding something that was lost
   b. finding something that nobody knew about before
   c. finding something in another country

4. The man who discovered the drink was John Zimmerman. He had a <u>clinic</u> where people could stay for one week to lose weight. A clinic is _____.
   a. a place where people go to learn something
   b. a place where people go to relax
   c. a place where people go to receive medical advice or treatment

5. If a person went to Mr. Zimmerman's clinic, Mr. Zimmerman <u>guaranteed</u> that the person would lose fourteen pounds. If the person didn't lose fourteen pounds, Mr. Zimmerman would give back the money he or she paid to come to the clinic. To guarantee something means to _____.
   a. make something better
   b. advertise something
   c. promise that something will work

6. Mr. Zimmerman was also <u>offering</u> a special price for one month only. The treatment would only cost $2,000 instead of $3,000. To offer something means to _____.
   a. provide it
   b. loan it
   c. keep it

7. My parents didn't want me to buy this treatment because it was <u>unproven</u>. When something is unproven it _____.
   a. can't be sold
   b. is inexpensive
   c. has not been shown to be true

8. I paid the $2,000 and received the drinks. Unfortunately, I didn't lose any weight at all. When I tried to call the clinic, I found out the phone had been disconnected. The clinic was not real, and the drink didn't work. The whole business was a <u>fraud</u>. An example of fraud is _____.
   a. helping people who are sick
   b. tricking people by lying to them
   c. learning how to cure people

9. The drink was <u>harmless</u>, but I lost $2,000! If something is harmless _____.
   a. it won't hurt you
   b. it isn't real
   c. it won't make you gain weight

10. And, unfortunately, the guarantee was also a <u>lie</u>. A lie is _____.
    a. something that is promised
    b. something that is true
    c. something that isn't true

11. Don't <u>make</u> the same <u>mistake</u> I did. Always ask your doctor or pharmacist before buying a new health product. To make a mistake is _____.
    a. to do something the wrong way
    b. to forget something
    c. to take something

2 Focus on Reading

Before you read the following article, discuss these questions with the class. Why is the title a question? What is "a miracle cure"?

A MIRACLE CURE?

from *Healthier You* magazine

1   One year ago, Matt Bloomfield was told he had cancer. His doctors decided to treat his cancer immediately. A few months after the treatments, however, Matt found out that the cancer was still growing. He became sick and depressed. Because he always had pain, the doctors gave him more medicine, but it didn't help. Finally, the doctors told him that they were unable to do anything more; he had only six months to live. Matt would do anything to save his life. He went to see a doctor who turned out to be a complete quack.

2   More and more people are turning away from their doctors and, instead, going to individuals who have no medical training and who sell unproven treatments. They go to quacks to get everything from treatments for colds to cures for cancer. And they are putting themselves in dangerous situations.

3   Many people don't realize how unsafe it is to use unproven treatments. First of all, the treatments usually don't work. They may be harmless, but if someone uses these products instead of proven treatments, he or she may be harmed. Why? Because during the time the person is using the product, his

or her illness may be getting worse. This can even cause the person to die.

4   So why do people trust quacks? People want the "miracle cure." They want the product that will solve their problem . . . quickly, easily, and completely. A patient may be so afraid of pain, or even of dying, that he or she will try anything. The quack knows this and offers an easy solution at a very high price.

5   Quacks usually sell products and treatments for illnesses that generally have no proven cure. This is why we often hear about clinics that treat cancer or AIDS. Treatments for arthritis[1] are also popular with quacks. Other common quackeries are treatments to lose weight quickly, to make hair grow again, and to keep a person young.

6   How can you recognize a quack? Sometimes it's easy because he or she offers something we know is impossible. A drink to keep you young is an example of this. But many times, these people lie, saying that their product was made because of a recent scientific discovery. This makes it more difficult to know if the product is real or a

---

[1] *arthritis:* a condition in which a person's joints are swollen and painful

fraud. Another way to recognize quackery is that many quacks will say their product is good for many different illnesses, not just for one thing. They usually like to offer money-back guarantees if their treatment doesn't work. Unfortunately, the guarantee is often also a lie. Finally, the fraudulent clinic will often be in another country. Laws in the United States make it illegal for a quack to have a clinic in the United States because the quack doesn't have the proper medical training.

7   Quacks try to sell their products in similar ways. They will invite you to read testimonials, letters written by satisfied customers. These frauds will also promise quick, exciting cures. Often they say the product is made in a secret way or with something secret in it which can only be bought from a particular company. Quacks will also say that doctors and the rest of the medical community are against them.

8   You are not powerless. There are things you can do to protect yourself from health fraud. Before you buy a product or treatment, check to see if it's the real thing. Talk to a doctor, pharmacist, or another health professional. If you've been the victim of health fraud, you can complain to certain organizations. In the United States, the Better Business Bureau, the Food and Drug Administration (FDA), the Federal Trade Commission, or the National Council against Health Fraud will help you.

9   Don't make the mistake of letting yourself or anyone you know become a victim of health fraud. It could cost you a lot of money or, worse yet, your life.

READING FOR MAIN IDEAS

Complete the main ideas below with the most appropriate word. On the right, note which paragraph in the reading the main idea came from.

Paragraph

1. Different quacks often try to sell their products in

_____*similar*_____ ways.   __7__

    a. similar   **b.** different   **c.** varied

2. It's _____ to use a quack's products.   _____

    a. fun   **b.** illegal   **c.** dangerous

3. Quacks want to sell products for illnesses that have no

_____ because their products don't really work.   _____

    a. medications   **b.** cure   **c.** side effects

4. If you are _____ about buying something from   _____
a quack, there are people and organizations that can help you.

    a. excited   **b.** worried   **c.** satisfied

5. There are many things a person can look for to determine if

a _____ is real or comes from a quack.   _____

    a. product   **b.** secret   **c.** salesman

6. People will often go to a quack because they want an easy
answer for their _____.   _____

    a. child   **b.** customer   **c.** problem

READING FOR DETAILS

Match the two parts of each sentence. Then match these details with the main idea they support from Reading for Main Ideas. Some main ideas are supported by more than one detail.

_g, 3_ **1.** Treatment for arthritis is a common quackery _____.

a. is by offering a quick solution to a problem

_____ **2.** Quacks often lie about their _____.

b. and will buy anything that might be a cure

_____ **3.** People go to quacks to get _____.

c. to be sure it's not a quackery

_____ **4.** You can ask a doctor about a product _____.

d. a variety of treatments

_____ **5.** Quacks understand that sick people are often afraid of death _____.

e. while using a quack's product

_____ **6.** A person's illness could get worse _____.

f. product or treatment

_____ **7.** One way that a quack gets customers _____.

g. because it doesn't have a proven cure

REACTING TO THE READING

1 *Think about what you learned in Reading One. Write **T** (true) or **F** (false) for each statement. Discuss your answers with the class.*

_____ **1.** Some unproven treatments really do work.

_____ **2.** Unproven treatments can make people worse.

_____ **3.** Quacks use people's fears to make money.

_____ **4.** People aren't likely to buy a quack's products if there is a money-back guarantee.

2 *Discuss the following questions with a partner.*

1. What would you have done if you were Matt Bloomfield?

2. What do you think government agencies can or cannot do for you in cases of fraud?

B **READING TWO:** *The Organic Health Center*

1 *Read the following advertisement about the Organic Health Center.*

THE Organic Health Center

1   Do you have cancer? Have the doctors given you no hope? I can help you. My name is Benjamin Harrison. I am the founder[1] of the Organic Health Center. My health center offers the most advanced treatments for curing cancer and other diseases.

2   After traveling around the world for nine years looking for a cure for myself, I was able to learn the causes of cancer. Now, I can help others by offering them a cure. This cure is available only at the Organic Health Center.

3   As a result of my experiences, I realized that Western doctors are unqualified to help their patients. I, on the other hand, have learned how to use the best herbs[2] and organic[3] foods to heal, and I *am* qualified[4] to help you. That's why doctors will tell you not to trust me. They know that I can do something they can't do.

4   My program focuses on the whole body. It works on the cause of the cancer. I will put you on the healthiest diet available. This diet uses the best herb and plant products I gathered from my travels around the world. All of the products I use are natural, so they won't make you feel sick. After one to six months on this diet, you will be cured of cancer.

5   Here are some of the programs my center offers:

PROGRAM A:	PROGRAM B:	PROGRAM C:
For all types of cancers	*For cancer detected early*	*For all other diseases*
Stay at my clinic for one month of treatment. Then continue the treatment in your home for two more months.	Complete a sixty-day program in your home. Eat a special diet with herbs and other healthy foods. Also follow an exercise schedule.	Complete a ninety-day program in your home. Eat a special diet with herbs and other healthy foods.

6   I am willing to travel to your home to teach you how to follow the program. And, if you would like, I have testimonial letters for you to read.

7   I provide a money-back guarantee if the program fails. Why? It is my guarantee to you that my treatment works.

2 *Answer the following questions. Then discuss your answers with a classmate.*

1. What is Reading Two about? Describe it in one sentence.

2. How is Benjamin Harrison qualified to cure people who have cancer?

3. How could you describe Harrison's treatment for cancer?

---

[1] *founder:* the person who started a program or an organization
[2] *herbs:* plants that can be used for cooking or medicine
[3] *organic:* grown naturally without chemicals
[4] *qualified:* to be properly trained in something

C LINKING READINGS ONE AND TWO

1 Look at "A Miracle Cure?" again. Find the different ways to identify a quack. List them on the left side of the chart. Then read "The Organic Health Center" again. Look for examples that show that Benjamin Harrison might be a quack. Make a list of those examples below. Give the paragraph number where you found the example.

ITEM FROM "A MIRACLE CURE?" THAT IDENTIFIES A QUACK	EXAMPLE OF THAT ITEM FOUND IN "THE ORGANIC HEALTH CENTER"
1. They treat illnesses that generally have no cure.	_1_ **1.** "My health center offers the most advanced treatments for curing cancer and other diseases."
2.	_____ **2.**
3.	_____ **3.**
4.	_____ **4.**
5.	_____ **5.**
6.	_____ **6.**
7.	_____ **7.**

2 *Below are several treatments for cancer. Which ones do you think are real treatments (R) and which ones are fraudulent (F)? Write your answers on the lines. Then discuss your answers with a partner.*

_____ 1. A diet based on a new scientific discovery. It must be followed strictly for three months. The diet includes fruits, vegetables, nuts, and grains. Animal products such as meat, eggs, milk, and cheese cannot be eaten.

_____ 2. A series of acupuncture treatments. These are taken until the cancer disappears completely.

_____ 3. Radiation treatment on the part of the body where the cancer is growing. These treatments must be taken every day for four weeks.

_____ 4. Herbal treatment that requires seven secret herbs to be cooked into the food at each meal. Meals must be taken six times a day until the cancer disappears.

_____ 5. Hormone treatment. This treatment increases the hormones in your body that fight against the cancer. It must be taken for five months.

_____ 6. A diet consisting only of breads, cheeses, fats, and wine. This must be followed strictly for five months until your body is clean.

_____ 7. Surgery to take out the part of the body with cancer. This is followed by four months of treatments using special medicines to kill any remaining cancer.

3 Focus on Vocabulary

1 *Look at the following sentences from Reading One. What do you notice about the words in italics? What do they have in common?*

Laws in the United States make it *il*legal for a quack to . . .
Many people don't realize how *un*safe it is to use *un*proven treatments.
You are not *powerless*.

The underlined parts of the words above are called prefixes if they come at the beginning of words, and suffixes if they come at the end of words. They can change the meaning of a word. For example, *legal, proven, safe,* and *power* all have positive meanings. *Illegal, unproven, unsafe,* and *powerless* all have negative meanings. The prefixes *il-* and *un-* mean "not." When you add *il-* to *legal,* the meaning changes to "not legal." When you add *un-* to *proven* and *safe,* the meaning changes to "not proven" and "not safe." *Power* has a positive meaning, but when you add the suffix *-less,* which means "without," the meaning becomes "without power," which is negative.

Look at the list of prefixes and suffixes. Then look at the words in the box, and circle those that have negative meanings.

Prefix	Meaning		Suffix	Meaning
un-	not		-less	without
ir-/il-/im-	not		-able/-ible	can be done
mis-	bad, fail			

im**proper**	**un**popular	hope**less**	**mis**understand
misused	lik**able**	un**able**	knowledge**able**
undecided	**ir**regular	help**less**	**ir**responsible

Do you know any other words in Reading One or Reading Two that could be made positive or negative by adding a prefix or suffix? List them below with their prefix or suffix.

_____	_____	_____	_____
_____	_____	_____	_____
_____	_____	_____	_____

2 *For each sentence, find the word in the box that has the same meaning as the underlined words. Then write each sentence using the word from the box. (You may need to change the form of the word to be grammatically correct.) The rest of the sentence should remain the same.*

harmless	guarantee	founder	victim of	~~offer~~
mistake	fraud	discovery	unproven	lie

1. The quack <u>provided</u> testimonials for interested people to read.

   The quack offered testimonials for interested people to read.

2. Even though many people believe that taking large amounts of vitamins can cure some diseases, this treatment is <u>not definitely true</u>.

   _____

3. The product came with a <u>paper that said it would definitely work</u>.

   _____

4. The <u>thing that nobody had ever seen before</u> was a new medicine from the rain forest.

   _____

5. Some telemarketers sell things that are a <u>lie</u>.

_____

6. "Quacks Anonymous" is an organization that helps victims of fraud. The <u>person who started it</u> is a successful businesswoman from California.

_____

7. Many cancer patients have made an <u>error</u> by using a quack's product that didn't work and delaying seeing a doctor.

_____

8. The <u>person who was harmed by</u> health fraud called the National Council against Health Fraud to report the quack.

_____

9. Many quack products are <u>not going to hurt anyone</u>.

_____

10. Quacks often <u>write or say something that isn't true</u> and say that their product is based on a recent scientific discovery.

_____

3 *Work in pairs. Student A, on a separate piece of paper write four questions using four of the words in the first column. Student B, write four questions using four of the words in the second column. Exchange papers, and write answers to each question using a word from below. Discuss your answers with your partner.*

Student A	Student B
miracle	harmless
quack	fraud
offer	clinic
qualified	guarantee
unproven	victim
discovery	mistake

Example

A: *Do you know anyone who has experienced a <u>miracle</u>?*

B: *Yes. My aunt was very sick and the doctors couldn't <u>offer</u> a cure, but she got better.*

4 Focus on Writing

A   STYLE: Summary Writing

1 *Reread "The Organic Health Center" on page 42. Then read the summary of "The Organic Health Center" below. The summary is written in the third person (**he/she/it**), but Reading Two is written in the first person (**I**). How else are they different?*

SUMMARY OF "THE ORGANIC HEALTH CENTER"

"The Organic Health Center" is an advertisement for a clinic to cure cancer. The founder is Benjamin Harrison, and he offers the most advanced treatments available. Through his travels, Harrison learned the causes and the cure of cancer. As a result, he knows what doctors don't know, and his treatments work. Using the healthiest diet with the best herbs and plant products available, he cures cancer. The clinic has several programs for different diseases, and they are all guaranteed.

A **summary** is a shorter version of a text. It helps the reader understand the most important information. There are several parts of a summary.

- It contains the main idea or topic of the text.

- It contains the important supporting details of the text. A supporting detail is a fact or example that helps explain the main idea.

- It contains definitions of important words.

- It doesn't contain the reader's opinions or other details.

- It is approximately one-fourth the length of the text.

---

2 *Work in small groups. Look at the sentences below. Read the topic sentence for "A Miracle Cure?" It contains the main idea of the article. The other sentences are important supporting details from "A Miracle Cure?" Together they form a summary, but they are out of order. Identify which supporting detail is first, second, third, and so on by looking back at Reading One. Label the sentences **SD1, SD2,** and so on.*

Topic Sentence: Many people are using quacks instead of doctors.

_____ 1. People often go to quacks because they want an easy solution for their problems and because they are afraid.

_____ 2. Quacks use similar techniques for selling their products.

_____ 3. It can be difficult to know if someone is a quack, but there are ways.

_____ 4. Quacks understand this. So they sell products for illnesses that have no cure, and people who are afraid of dying will pay any price for them.

_____ 5. If you are concerned about buying something from a quack, there are people and organizations that can help you.

_____ 6. Unfortunately, these people often don't realize how dangerous it is to use a quack. It is dangerous because the product usually doesn't work. As a result, the patient's illness can be getting worse during the treatment.

Now write the topic sentence and the supporting-detail sentences in order on a separate piece of paper so that you have a summary for "A Miracle Cure?"

3 *In summary writing, it is important to reread your summary and edit it. One of the ways to do this is to add transitions to make it flow. Look at the transition words below. Circle them in the summary you just wrote.*

as a result	so	also	unfortunately

Now write a summary paragraph of what you have learned about how to prevent quackery and fraud. Use what you have learned in Readings One and Two and in discussions with your classmates. Exchange your finished summary with a partner. Check that your partner has used transition words in the summary.

B GRAMMAR: Adjectives—Superlatives

1 *Look at the pairs of sentences below. How are they different?*

1. **a.** The founder is Benjamin Harrison, and he offers <u>advanced</u> treatments.
   b. The founder is Benjamin Harrison, and he offers <u>the most advanced</u> treatments available.

2. **a.** Using a <u>healthy</u> diet with <u>good</u> herbs and plant products, he cures cancer.
   b. Using <u>the healthiest</u> diet with <u>the best</u> herbs and plant products available, he cures cancer.

Superlatives of Adjectives

We use the superlative form of the adjective when we are comparing two or more things and when we want to emphasize that one of the things has an exceptional quality. Imagine, for example, that there are three herb products on sale. One costs two dollars, one costs five dollars, and one costs ten dollars. The two-dollar product is **the least expensive** one. The ten-dollar product is **the most expensive** one.

There are different ways to form the superlative.

1. For most one-syllable adjectives and for two-syllable adjectives that end in *-y,* use *the* + **adjective** + *-est.* For adjectives ending in *-y,* change the *-y* to *-i* before adding *-est.*

tall	the tallest
happy	the happiest
dark	the darkest
healthy	the healthiest

I will put you on **the healthiest** diet available.

2. For most adjectives with two or more syllables, use *the most / the least* + **adjective.**

advanced	the most advanced
beautiful	the most beautiful
intelligent	the most intelligent

The founder is Benjamin Harrison, and he offers **the most advanced** treatments available.

3. There are also some irregular superlative forms.

good	the best
bad	the worst
little	the least
far	the farthest/the furthest

I, on the other hand, have learned how to use **the best** herbs and organic food to heal.

2 *Look at the following testimonial for the Organic Health Center. Complete the sentences with the superlative forms of the adjectives in parentheses. Don't forget to use **the**.*

To Whom It May Concern:

In 1997, I was diagnosed with cancer. I went through the treatments the doctors ordered. The doctors promised me I was getting better. But I could tell that I wasn't. My health was _____ it had ever been.
1. (bad)

Then I heard of Benjamin Harrison's Organic Health Center. I talked with him and asked him many questions. After talking with Harrison, I could tell that he was _____ of anyone I had talked to.
2. (educated)

It became clearer and clearer to me that using Western medicine was not _____ way to treat my cancer.
3. (intelligent)

I decided to try Harrison's cure for cancer. After only two weeks, I felt much better. And Harrison's cure was _____ treatment of all the ones I tried.
4. (easy)

I would like everyone who reads this letter to know that I was cured after only three months. It has now been ten months, and my health is _____
5. (good)
it's ever been. My doctors say that my recovery is _____ they have
6. (fast)
ever seen. This is because Harrison is _____ health professional
7. (dedicated)
I know.

I want to thank Benjamin Harrison for being _____ person I
8. (helpful)
met during my illness. Without his help, I might not be alive today! If you have cancer, contact Benjamin Harrison immediately. You deserve to be _____ person you can be.
9. (healthy)

Sincerely,

Cheryl B.

C WRITING TOPICS

Choose one of the following topics. Write two or three paragraphs using some of the vocabulary, grammar, and style you learned in this unit.

1. Write your own advertisement for a fraudulent product. Use pictures or illustrations to make it look like a real ad.

2. Most cultures have traditional treatments that have been used for many years. These treatments may not be scientific, but they seem to work. Explain how these treatments are both similar to and different from fraudulent cures.

3. Imagine that you have cancer. You have tried every medical treatment the doctors have recommended, and you are still getting worse. The doctors say they cannot help you anymore. Would you try a product or treatment that could be a quackery? Summarize what you know about quackery. Then consider the advantages and disadvantages of using quacks, and make a decision.

4. Do you think it is wrong for a quack to offer hope to someone who has been told he or she is dying? Why or why not?

D RESEARCH TOPIC

Work in small groups to look at advertisements in magazines or on the Internet. (Especially look at sports, fashion, and health magazines.) Start at the back of the magazine since many ads are found there.

Step 1: Find one or two advertisements that you think may show fraudulent products, and complete the information below.

- Type of product or treatment: _____

- What the product is supposed to do: _____

- Reasons why this may be fraudulent:

  _____

  _____

  _____

  _____

- Do you think people will buy this product? Why or why not? _____

  _____

- If your answer to the question above was *yes*, what kind of person would buy this product?

  _____

Step 2: Share your information with a small group of classmates. Discuss what kinds of products seem to be popular with quacks. Write a one-paragraph report summarizing your group's findings.

For step-by-step practice in the writing process, see *Writing Activity Book, Intermediate,* Unit 3.

Assignment	Summary and Response Paragraphs
Prewriting	Responding to a Reading
Organizing	Summarizing
Revising	Using Transitions
	Using Superlative Adjectives
Editing	Using Commas and Periods

For Unit 3 Internet activities, visit the NorthStar Companion Website at
http://www.longman.com/northstar.

The Metamorphosis

1 Focus on the Topic

A PREDICTING

1. Look at the photograph of the cockroach. Work in small groups. Write as many adjectives as you can to describe the cockroach and your feelings about it.

2. Read the title of the unit. *Metamorphosis* means a process in which something changes completely into something else. What do you think this unit will be about?

B   SHARING INFORMATION

Work in small groups. Discuss the following questions.

1. What kinds of insects are you afraid of? What kinds of insects do you like?

2. Have you ever had a bad dream about an insect? Explain.

3. Do you know of any insects that people like to eat? Which ones?

4. Movies about insects, such as *A Bug's Life,* have been successful. Why do you think people like this type of movie?

C   PREPARING TO READ

BACKGROUND

Read about Franz Kafka, the author of the story in Reading One.

Franz Kafka was born in Prague (in the Czech Republic) on July 3, 1883. He was the only son, and he had three younger sisters. His father was a very large, strong man with a powerful personality. His mother was quieter. She was a thinker. Franz was like his mother. He was very small and skinny, and he had a weak personality. He was a thinker. He always felt that he was a disappointment to his father. Although he was engaged many times, he never got married. He died of tuberculosis at age forty.

Based on the text, do you agree or disagree with the following statements? Discuss your opinion with the class.

1. Franz had a good relationship with his father.

2. Franz thought he would be a weak husband, so he never married.

3. He always compared himself to his father.

VOCABULARY FOR COMPREHENSION

1 *Guess the meaning of the underlined words in the sentences. Write your own definition, or synonym, on the line. Then compare your answers with your classmates'.*

1. My parents <u>supported</u> me until I finished college, but then I had to get a job and pay for everything by myself.

   paid for what I needed

2. When she saw the spider, she <u>fainted</u> and fell down on the floor.

3. The thief <u>grabbed</u> the woman's purse and ran away with it.

4. Someone was <u>beating</u> on the door, and the loud noise woke up everyone in the house.

5. Some people don't want to get close to insects or touch them because they really don't like them. They think insects are <u>disgusting</u>.

6. Many smokers wish that they could remove the bad <u>substance</u> from cigarettes. Then they could smoke without worrying about their health.

7. After the bee stung the child, he screamed and cried loudly. His mother held him in her arms and sang to him, and this finally <u>soothed</u> him enough to fall asleep.

8. Firefighters are very <u>brave</u> when they go into burning buildings to save people.

9. Some people enjoy a good, <u>smelly</u> cheese like blue cheese. Others don't like the smell and won't eat it.

10. He has very strong legs because he runs five miles every day, but his arms are almost <u>useless</u>; he can't lift anything heavy at all.

_____

11. It took a long time, but I finally <u>managed to</u> finish my degree and graduate.

_____

12. I didn't <u>realize</u> how difficult it was to ski until I tried it.

_____

2 *Match each word with a synonym or phrase. Compare your answers with a partner's.*

_____	**1.** support	**a.** take something quickly and roughly
_____	**2.** faint	**b.** not afraid of danger
_____	**3.** grab	**c.** relieve
_____	**4.** realize	**d.** succeed in doing something difficult
_____	**5.** disgusting	**e.** anything one can touch
_____	**6.** substance	**f.** hit repeatedly
_____	**7.** soothe	**g.** provide the money someone needs to live
_____	**8.** brave	**h.** strongly disliked
_____	**9.** smelly	**i.** having a bad odor
_____	**10.** useless	**j.** lose consciousness, as if you were asleep
_____	**11.** manage to	**k.** not working well or of no use
_____	**12.** beat	**l.** start to know something you had not noticed before

2 Focus on Reading

A   READING ONE: *The Metamorphosis*

The following paragraph is from the story you are going to read. As you read, think about the picture of the cockroach on page 53. Then answer the questions.

Well, it was time to get up. Surely, as soon as he got out of bed, he would realize this had all been a bad dream. He tried to move his back part out first, but it moved so slowly, and he had a hard time. His thin little legs seemed useless, just moving and moving in the air, not helping him at all. Then he tried the front part. This worked better, but he still couldn't move enough to get out of bed. He began rocking back and forth, stronger and stronger, and finally threw himself onto the floor, hitting his head as he fell.

1. Something has happened to this man. Why is it so hard for him to get out of bed?

   _____

   _____

   _____

2. What does this sentence mean: "Surely, as soon as he got out of bed, he would realize this had all been a bad dream"?

   _____

   _____

   _____

3. What do you think the rest of the story will be about?

   _____

   _____

   _____

THE
METAMORPHOSIS

FRANZ KAFKA

1   One morning, Gregor Samsa woke up from a bad dream and realized he was some kind of terrible insect. He was a cockroach, and he was as large as a man! Lying on his back, he could see his large brown belly and thin legs. He tried to turn over onto his side, but every time he tried, he would roll onto his back again.

2   He began to think about his job as a traveling salesman. He hated his job, but he had to do it to support his father, mother, and sister because his father no longer worked. He looked at the clock and realized he had overslept—it was 6:30! He was late. The next train left at 7:00. He would have to hurry to make it. A few minutes later his mother yelled to him: "It's 6:45. You're late. Get up!" When he answered her, he was surprised to hear his voice; it sounded so high. "Yes, mother. I'm getting up now." His sister now whispered through the door, "Gregor, are you all right? Do you need anything?"

3   Well, it was time to get up. Surely, as soon as he got out of bed, he would realize this had all been a bad dream. He tried to move his back part out first, but it moved so slowly, and he had a hard time. His thin little legs seemed useless, just moving and moving in the air, not helping him at all. Then he tried the front part. This worked better, but he still couldn't move enough to get out of bed. He began rocking back and forth, stronger and stronger, and finally threw himself onto the floor, hitting his head as he fell.

4   All of a sudden, he heard a knock at the door. It was his manager, who had come to see why he was late. "Oh," thought Gregor, "I hate my job." Then the manager spoke. "Mr. Samsa, I must warn you that you could lose your job because of this. Lately, your work has not been very good, and now I find you in bed when you should be at work!" Gregor panicked and said, "No, no, I will come out immediately. I was sick, but now I feel much better." The manager and Gregor's family did not understand a single word he said, for his speech was now the hiss of an insect. As he talked, he managed to move himself to the chest of drawers, tried to stand up, then slipped and fell, holding tightly to a chair with his thin legs. He finally managed to open the door to talk to his manager.

5   At the sight of him, the manager screamed, his mother fainted, and his father wept. The manager began to back out of the room to leave, and Gregor realized he couldn't let him go. He let go of the door and dropped into the living room on his tiny little legs. Again his mother screamed,

while the manager disappeared out the door. His father quickly grabbed a walking stick and a newspaper to beat Gregor back into his bedroom. Once Gregor was inside, the door was locked from the outside.

6   Gregor awoke as it was getting dark. He smelled food and saw that his sister, Grete, had left him one of his favorite meals, a bowl of milk with bread in it. But, when he tasted it, it tasted terrible, and he turned away in disgust. He slid under the couch and slept there until morning.

7   The next morning, Gregor's sister looked in and was surprised to see that he hadn't eaten a thing. She picked up the bowl and soon returned with some old vegetables, bones, and smelly cheese, which she offered to him. After she left, Gregor hungrily ate them all up. And so the days passed, for she was the only one brave enough to come into the room.

8   Gregor grew tired of being in the bedroom day and night, and soon took to walking back and forth across the walls and ceiling. It felt much better than walking on the floor. His sister noticed this because of the brown sticky substance left from his feet wherever he walked. She decided to move most of the furniture out of the room to make more walking space for Gregor. But Gregor wanted to keep a picture on the wall—a picture of a beautiful woman dressed in pretty clothes. While Grete and her mother were in the other room, he quickly climbed the wall and pressed himself against the picture to stop them from taking it. When his mother saw him, she screamed and fainted. His sister then became very angry with him. He followed her into the dining room to help her, but this frightened her. When his father returned home and learned what had happened, he became very angry. Gregor tried to return to his bedroom to get away from his father, but was unsuccessful. He couldn't fit through the doorway. Suddenly, his father started throwing apples at him. The first few didn't hurt him, but then one pierced his body, and he felt terrible pain. His mother rushed over to his father to beg him not to kill Gregor, as Gregor slowly crawled back to his room.

9   The apple remained in Gregor's back and stopped him from being able to walk easily. This gave him great pain. His sister also began to care less and less about feeding him and cleaning his room. Well, he wasn't very hungry anyway. The dust and dirt gradually became thick on the floor and stuck to him whenever he moved.

10   The family now left his door to the dining room open for two hours every night after dinner, and he could listen to their conversation. He really loved this. One night, they forgot to lock Gregor's door. When his sister began to play the violin, which she had not done for a long time, he felt so good. The music was beautiful and soothing. He had begun to walk toward her to tell her how wonderful it was, when his family saw him. The music suddenly stopped. Grete became very upset. "Momma, Poppa," she said, "This cannot go on. We must find a way to get rid of this thing. It is destroying our lives."

11   Gregor slowly crawled back to his room. He lay there in the dark and couldn't move. Even the place in his back where the apple was no longer hurt. He thought of his family tenderly as he lay there, and, when the light began to come through the window, he died.

12   When Gregor was found dead the next morning, the whole family seemed to feel relieved. For the first time in a long, long time, they went out and took a train ride to the country, making plans for the future.

Abridged from "The Metamorphosis," by Franz Kafka (1883–1924).

READING FOR MAIN IDEAS

Read the main ideas from the story. They are all false in some way. Rewrite each main idea so that it is correct.

1. Gregor dreams he has become an insect.

_____

2. His family thinks it's funny when they see Gregor.

_____

3. Only his mother takes care of him, and she eventually stops.

_____

4. He dies in the living room as he thinks of his job.

_____

5. His family feels helpless when he dies.

_____

READING FOR DETAILS

To paraphrase *a sentence means to say it in a different way, using your own words. The sentences below are paraphrases of sentences in the story. Write the exact sentence from the story that has the same meaning as each of the sentences below. The first one has been done for you.*

1. His sister wanted to know if he was OK.

His sister now whispered through the door, "Gregor, are you all right? Do
you need anything?"

2. Because he was very afraid, he promised to come out of his room quickly.

_____

_____

3. The manager felt afraid and tried to leave carefully, and Gregor knew he must stop him.

_____

_____

4. He moved easily and quietly under the sofa and stayed there until the next day.

_____

_____

5. His sister was amazed early the next day when she noticed he had not touched his food.

_____

_____

6. At first they didn't hurt him, but then one cut into him and hurt him badly.

_____

_____

7. Gradually, his sister lost interest in taking care of him.

_____

_____

8. It was time to think of how to remove him.

_____

_____

REACTING TO THE READING

1 _Write **T** (true) or **F** (false) for each statement. If you mark **T**, find an example in the text to support the statement, and write it on the line._

_____ 1. In the beginning of the story, Grete loved her brother and cared about him.

_____

_____ **2.** Gregor wanted to be an insect so that he wouldn't have to go to work.

_____

_____ **3.** Gregor was really afraid that he was going to lose his job when the manager came to his house.

_____

_____ **4.** Gregor's family was afraid of him.

_____

_____ **5.** Gregor was very lonely.

_____

_____ **6.** Grete stopped thinking of Gregor as a person and thought of him only as a disgusting cockroach.

_____

2 *Write answers to the questions below on a separate piece of paper. Then discuss your answers with the class.*

1. Did the story turn out the way you expected it to? Look back at your ideas about the story on page 57. Compare your predictions with the story.

2. Do you think this is a funny story? a sad story? a happy story? Explain.

3. Why do you think Kafka chose to have Gregor turn into a cockroach? Why not an animal?

4. What kind of relationship does Gregor have with his family? How does that affect Gregor's feelings about himself?

5. What is your opinion of Gregor at the end of the story? Do you see him the same way his family does?

B   READING TWO: *Ungeziefer*

1 *Many critics* *have studied Kafka's stories. Read the following explanation of "The Metamorphosis." Think about what Kafka was trying to say in this story.*

---

* *critics:* people who give opinions about the quality of things, especially the arts, such as paintings, literature, and music

UNGEZIEFER

1   "The Metamorphosis" is a short story which is both funny and sad at the same time. It is funny because of how Gregor must learn to move his new "cockroach" legs and body. On the other hand, it is sad because he loses the love of his family as a result of his becoming so disgusting.

2   Why did Kafka choose to tell a story about a man who turns into a cockroach? Certainly many people are afraid of cockroaches and other insects. They think cockroaches are ugly and disgusting. Why would Kafka choose something that most of us hate? What was his purpose?

3   Many critics have written their ideas about Kafka's purpose. One explanation comes from a word that Kafka used in his story. Kafka wrote his story in German, and he used the German word *ungeziefer,* or vermin,[1] which can be used to mean a person who is rough and disgusting. In English, we do the same thing. If we call a person a "cockroach," we mean that the person is weak and cowardly.[2] Gregor, the man, is like a cockroach. He is weak and disgusting. Why? Because he doesn't want to be the supporter of his family. He hates his job and wishes he didn't have to do it in order to pay off the family debt.[3] In addition, his family has been like a parasite[4] to him. Gregor's family members have all enjoyed relaxing, not working, while he alone has had to work. When he becomes a cockroach, he becomes the parasite to the family. So Gregor's true self is metamorphosed into an insect because his true self wants to be like a child again, helpless and having no responsibility.

4   Another explanation comes from Kafka's relationship with his father. Kafka was a small, quiet man. He saw himself as weak and spineless compared to his father, who was physically large and had a powerful personality. It is the same with Gregor. He also sees himself as a failure. By turning himself into an insect, Gregor is able to rebel against his father and, at the same time, punish himself for rebelling. This punishment results in his being physically and emotionally separated from his family with no hope of joining them again, and finally he dies.

5   Kafka's choice of an insect makes this story work because many people feel insects are disgusting. Gregor becomes the vermin, the disgusting son that nobody cares about. His family rejects him because of his appearance, yet he continues to love them to the end.

---

[1] *vermin:* small, wild animals, like rats, that can carry diseases and are difficult to control
[2] *cowardly:* afraid, easily frightened
[3] *debt:* money that you owe to someone
[4] *parasite:* an animal or plant that lives in or on another animal or plant and gets its food from it

2 *Answer these questions on a separate piece of paper.*

1. Do the critics think this is a funny story, a sad story, or a happy story? Why?

2. Why do the critics think Kafka chose to have Gregor turn into a cockroach, not an animal?

3. What kind of relationship do the critics think Gregor had with his family, and how did that affect his feelings about himself?

4. What is the critics' opinion of Gregor at the end of the story?

C   LINKING READINGS ONE AND TWO

Now compare the critics' ideas with your own ideas in Reacting to the Reading, Exercise 2 (p. 62). Were you as critical of Gregor as the professional critics? Were you less critical?

3 Focus on Vocabulary

1 *Look at the pairs of sentences below from "The Metamorphosis." What do you notice about the relationship between the underlined words?*

1. a. He <u>began</u> to think about his job as a traveling salesman.

   b. He <u>started</u> to think about his job as a traveling salesman.

2. a. He hated his <u>job</u>, but he had to do it to support his father, mother, and sister because his father no longer worked.

   b. He hated his <u>work</u>, but he had to do it to support his father, mother, and sister because his father no longer worked.

The pairs of words above are called **synonyms** because they have a similar meaning. A synonym might also give a more specific or precise meaning of a word. For example, *knocking on the door* is more specific than *hitting the door.*

2 *Look at the following pairs of sentences. Compare sentence **b** with sentence **a** in each item. How does the meaning change when you use a different synonym? Circle your opinion about the new meaning for each pair of sentences. Then discuss the variation in meanings with the class.*

1. a. One morning, Gregor Samsa woke up from a bad dream and <u>realized</u> he was some kind of terrible insect.

   b. One morning, Gregor Samsa woke up from a bad dream and <u>understood</u> he was some kind of terrible insect.

   New meaning: Similar   More General   More Specific

2. **a.** <u>Surely</u>, as soon as he got out of bed, he would realize this had all been a bad dream.

   b. <u>Certainly</u>, as soon as he got out of bed, he would realize this had all been a bad dream.

   New meaning: Similar   More General   More Specific

3. **a.** All of a sudden, he heard a <u>knock</u> at the door.

   b. All of a sudden, he heard a <u>tap</u> at the door.

   New meaning: Similar   More General   More Specific

4. **a.** The manager and Gregor's family did not <u>understand</u> a single word he said, for his speech was now the hiss of an insect.

   b. The manager and Gregor's family did not <u>comprehend</u> a single word he said, for his speech was now the hiss of an insect.

   New meaning: Similar   More General   More Specific

5. **a.** At the sight of him, the manager screamed, his mother fainted, and his father <u>wept</u>.

   b. At the sight of him, the manager screamed, his mother fainted, and his father <u>cried</u>.

   New meaning: Similar   More General   More Specific

6. **a.** But, when he tasted it, it tasted <u>terrible</u>, and he turned away in disgust.

   b. But, when he tasted it, it tasted <u>awful</u>, and he turned away in disgust.

   New meaning: Similar   More General   More Specific

7. **a.** She picked up the bowl and soon returned with some old vegetables, bones, and <u>smelly</u> cheese, which she offered to him.

   b. She picked up the bowl and soon returned with some old vegetables, bones, and <u>stinky</u> cheese, which she offered to him.

   New meaning: Similar   More General   More Specific

8. **a.** The first few didn't hurt him, but then one <u>pierced</u> his body, and he felt terrible pain.

   b. The first few didn't hurt him, but then one <u>entered</u> his body, and he felt terrible pain.

   New meaning: Similar   More General   More Specific

3 *Complete the crossword puzzle. Read the clues below, and choose words from the box.*

beat	grab	soothed
~~brave~~	managed to	useless
cockroach	metamorphosis	
couch	screamed	

Across

2. I think that people who are not afraid of snakes are very _____.

4. It was difficult, but she _____ finish her research paper on time.

6. The baby was _____ by the soft music.

9. A caterpillar changing into a butterfly is one stage in the process of _____.

10. Hurry up! _____ your coat and let's go.

Down

1. They _____ when they saw all the cockroaches on the floor.

3. I'm going to rest on the _____ and watch TV.

5. The most disgusting insect is a _____.

7. This old bicycle is _____. The gears are broken.

8. The musician in the marching band _____ the drum loudly.

4 *Write short answers to the following questions. Use the underlined words in your answers. Then share your responses with the class.*

1. Have you ever broken your arm or leg or some other part of your body? How did you feel when that part of your body was <u>useless</u>? Did you need to have help from others?

   _____

   _____

2. In your culture, how long do parents usually <u>support</u> their children? Until they finish high school? graduate from a university? get married? buy a house?

   _____

   _____

3. What insects do you think are <u>disgusting</u>? Why?

   _____

   _____

4. Can you think of a sticky <u>substance</u>? a smelly <u>substance</u>? a rough <u>substance</u>? Write them here.

   _____

   _____

5. Can you think of a famous person or someone you know who is <u>brave</u>? Write something about that person.

   _____

   _____

6. What foods from your country are <u>smelly</u>? Do you like them? Why or why not? Do you think someone from another country would like them? Why or why not?

   _____

   _____

4 Focus on Writing

A STYLE: Paraphrasing

To **paraphrase** a sentence means to say it in a different way, using your own words. The meaning of the original sentence doesn't change, but the words do. You can paraphrase sentences by using synonyms or by wording phrases differently. Look at the following sentences from the reading, and notice how they have been changed.

Original:	I **hate** my job.
Paraphrase:	I **don't like** my job.
Original:	It was his **manager,** who had come **to see** why he was late.
Paraphrase:	It was his **boss,** who had come **to find out** why he was late.
Original:	**Lately,** your work has **not been very good.**
Paraphrase:	**Recently,** your work has **been bad.**

1 *Paraphrase the sentences below. Replace the underlined word or words in the original sentence with a synonym or phrase that has a similar meaning.*

1. I was sick, but now I feel <u>much better</u>.

   I was sick, but now I feel fine.
   _____

2. The <u>manager began</u> to back out of the room to leave.

   _____

3. But, when he <u>tasted</u> it, it tasted <u>terrible</u>, and he turned away in disgust.

   _____

4. And so the days passed, for she was the only one brave enough <u>to come into</u> the room.

   _____

5. His mother ran to his father <u>to beg</u> him not to <u>kill</u> Gregor.

   _____

2 *Paraphrase the sentences or phrases below. You can replace any of the words or phrases. Make sure that your paraphrase has the same meaning as the original.*

1. Yes, Mother. I'm getting up now.

   _____

2. . . . because his father no longer worked.

   _____

3. The manager and Gregor's family did not understand a single word he said.

   _____

4. This cannot go on.

   _____

5. Again his mother screamed, while the manager disappeared out the door.

   _____

B   GRAMMAR: Infinitives of Purpose

1 *Read the following sentences. Underline the verbs that have the form **to + verb**. What questions do these verbs answer?*

1. Gregor worked to support his family.
2. His sister whispered to him to ask if he was all right.
3. He rocked back and forth to get out of bed.

Infinitives of Purpose

Look at the questions and answers below.

Questions	Answers
Why did Gregor work?	He had **to support** his family.
Why did his sister whisper to him?	She wanted **to ask** if he was all right.
Why did he rock back and forth?	He rocked back and forth **in order to get out of bed.**

(continued)

1. Infinitives that are used to explain the purpose of an action are called **infinitives of purpose.** They answer the question "Why?"

Gregor worked **to support** his family.

His sister whispered to him **to ask** if he was all right.

2. You can also use the longer form **in order to + verb.**

Gregor worked **in order to support** his family.

His sister whispered to him **in order to ask** if he was all right.

2 *Match the questions on the left with the answers on the right.*

Questions

_d_ 1. Why did Gregor's manager come to his house?

___ 2. Why was Gregor locked in his room?

___ 3. Why did his father grab a walking stick and newspaper?

___ 4. Why did Grete go into Gregor's room every day?

___ 5. Why did Gregor follow Grete into the dining room?

___ 6. Why did Gregor come out of his room?

___ 7. Why did his family take a train ride?

Answers

a. She needed to feed him.

b. He wanted to listen to the music.

c. He wanted to help her.

d. He wanted to see why Gregor was late.

e. They wanted to celebrate his death.

f. His family wanted to keep him there.

g. He wanted to beat Gregor.

3 *Now combine the questions and answers to make sentences that answer the question "Why"?*

1. *Gregor's manager came to his house to see why he was late.*

2. _____

3. _____

4. _____

5. _____

6. _____

7. _____

C WRITING TOPICS

Choose one of the following topics. Write two or three paragraphs, using some of the vocabulary, grammar, and style you learned in this unit.

1. Choose a short story from your home country about insects or animals, and write it in English. Or, use your imagination to write your own short story about insects or animals.

2. Explain your reaction to "The Metamorphosis." Did you like the story or not? Why? Which character in the story was the most interesting to you? Why?

3. Horror movies are very popular. Why do you think people like to watch them? Include examples of popular horror movies.

D RESEARCH TOPICS

1. Animal or insect story

Go to the library or a local bookstore and find a short story about an animal or insect to read. Draw or paint a large illustration of the story. Give an oral presentation about the story you chose. You might like to explain the title, say what country the story comes from, and then tell the story.

2. Metamorphosis of an insect or a frog

Read about the metamorphosis of an insect, such as a butterfly, or an amphibian, such as a frog. Write about the metamorphosis process by paraphrasing, not copying, the information. Make a diagram of the metamorphosis process. Submit a copy of the original text with your report so your teacher can check your paraphrasing. Give a presentation of your information to the class.

For step-by-step practice in the writing process, see *Writing Activity Book, Intermediate,* Unit 4.

Assignment	Folktale
Prewriting	Freewriting
Organizing	Telling a Story with a Moral
Revising	Writing Dialogue
	Using Infinitives of Purpose
Editing	Using Quotation Marks

For Unit 4 Internet activities, visit the NorthStar Companion Website at http://www.longman.com/northstar.

Speaking of Gender

1 Focus on the Topic

A PREDICTING

Look at the photograph, and discuss these questions with the class.

1. Do you think the baby is a boy or a girl? Why?

2. Read the title of the unit. What is gender?

B SHARING INFORMATION

Often boys and girls are given different types of toys, games, and clothing. Complete the chart below about your home culture. In the Boys column, list items that only boys play with or use. In the Girls column, list items that only girls play with or use. In the last column, write items that both boys and girls use. Share your chart with another student and then with the class.

Example

Home culture: _The United States_

	Boys	Girls	Both
Toys	Truck	Doll	Kite

Your home culture: _____

	Boys	Girls	Both
Toys			
Games			
Clothing			

C PREPARING TO READ

BACKGROUND

*Write **A** (agree) or **D** (disagree) next to each statement. When you are finished, compare your answers with a classmate's.*

_____ 1. Boys and girls are treated differently even before they are born.

_____ 2. From birth, a child knows how to behave as a male or female.

_____ 3. In my culture, it's better to be a boy.

_____ 4. In my culture, it's better to be a girl.

_____ 5. Boys and girls like different games.

_____ 6. Men and women have different ways of speaking.

_____ 7. Men's friendships with other men are different from women's friendships with other women.

VOCABULARY FOR COMPREHENSION

Look at the three choices below each sentence. Cross out the one that is not a synonym of the underlined word in the sentence.

1. Even though Sara is only six years old, she is already so <u>feminine</u>. Her dress and her hair are soft and pretty. She is so polite, carefully saying "please" and "thank you" at just the right time.

   a. girlish   **b.** ladylike   **c.** ~~proud~~

2. In North American culture, most people think a cowboy is very <u>masculine</u>. He has male characteristics, such as strength and courage.

   a. soft   **b.** tough   **c.** bold

3. For most people, their gender is an important part of who they are (or how they act). It is an important part of their <u>identity</u>.

   a. self   **b.** wealth   **c.** role

4. Language <u>reflects</u> the culture of the people that speak it. You can't understand a people's language if you don't understand their culture.

   a. shows   **b.** expresses   **c.** confuses

5. The children <u>competed</u> in a contest. They wanted to see who could jump rope the most times in a row and not miss.

   a. tried to win   **b.** tried to be the best   **c.** tried to help each other

6. When a boy is playing with a ball and will not give it to his sister, she might say "You're not playing <u>fairly</u>. Play fair. It's my turn."

   a. with tricks   **b.** by sharing equally   **c.** by the rules

7. Parents <u>influence</u> the way their children think and act. Children learn a lot from them.

   a. guide   **b.** ignore   **c.** change

8. American culture <u>emphasizes</u> success for men and beauty for women.

   a. gives frequently   **b.** gives importance to   **c.** gives value to

9. Many people think that a man gains <u>status</u> by marrying a beautiful woman, and a woman gains <u>status</u> by marrying a successful man.

   a. trouble in society   **b.** power in society   **c.** importance in society

10. People sometimes like to <u>gossip</u> about other people.

    a. talk about secrets   **b.** talk about behavior   **c.** talk about movies

11. In some cultures, having many children <u>proves</u> a man is masculine.

    a. shows clearly   **b.** shows frequently   **c.** shows to be true

2 Focus on Reading

A READING ONE: *Different Ways of Talking*

Read the first paragraph of the reading. Then write your answers to the following questions.

1. How did Joy's parents respond to the news that they were having a girl? What did they do? _____

_____

_____

_____

2. What did their friends and relatives do? What other things could they have done? _____

_____

_____

_____

3. Look at the reading title. Look back at your answers to questions 1 and 2. Predict what the reading will be about. Write your ideas here.

_____

_____

_____

_____

_____

_____

_____

Discuss your ideas with the class. Then continue reading "Different Ways of Talking."

Different Ways of Talking

1   A few hours after Joy Fisher's birth, her parents took pictures of her. Joy's mother put a pink headband around Joy's head, so that everyone who saw the pictures would know that the new baby was a girl. Even before she was born, Joy's parents knew that she was going to be female. When Joy's mother was six months pregnant, she got a sonogram, or picture of the baby. When the doctor said, "I'm sure you have a little lady in there," Joy's parents told all their relatives and friends that their baby was a girl. Gifts soon arrived, including pink dresses and dolls. Joy's parents decorated her room in pink and white.

2   A few years later, Joy's brother, Tommy, was born. His room was painted blue, and he received books and a football as gifts. Joy enjoyed helping her mother take care of the new baby. She also enjoyed playing with other girls at school. Now, Tommy has also entered school, where he plays with other boys. The games Joy and Tommy play are quite different. Joy loves jumping rope with her two best friends. Tommy likes to play ball with a large group of boys. Sometimes when they play a game, he is the captain. He enjoys telling the other boys what to do. Joy, on the other hand, doesn't like it when new girls join her friends and try to change the way they jump rope. She thinks that some of these girls are too bossy.

3   Both Joy and Tommy are growing up in the culture of the United States. They are learning what it means to be a girl and a boy in this culture. Their sex at birth, female and male, is now becoming a gender—a way of

thinking, speaking, and acting that is considered feminine or masculine. Each culture has its own way of defining gender, and very early in life gender becomes a basic part of a person's identity. According to Deborah Tannen, a professor at Georgetown University, gender differences are even reflected in the ways that men and women use language. Tannen and others who study communication believe that these differences begin early in life.

4   For example, in the United States and Canada, boys and girls usually play in same-

sex groups. Boys might play in large groups in which every boy knows his place. Some are leaders; others are followers. Boys compete with one another for leadership. Many boys like to get attention by boasting, or talking about how well they can do things. The games that they play often have complicated rules, and each boy tries hard to win.

5   Girls, in contrast, usually play in smaller groups. Sometimes they play with only one or two "best friends." Most girls want other girls to like them, and this is more important to them than winning. Girls may be interested

in playing fairly and taking turns. For example, when girls jump rope together, two girls hold the rope while others jump. Then the rope-holders take their turn jumping.

6   Tannen has found that these differences are reflected in the ways that children use language while they play. Boys often use commands when they talk to each other. For instance, when Tommy is captain he might say, "You go first. Don't wait for me." As the leader of the other boys, he tells them exactly what to do. But when Joy wants to influence her friends, she uses different forms of language. Instead of using commands, she will say, "Let's try it this way. Let's do this." This is how she tries to direct the other girls without sounding bossy. By using the form "let's," she also emphasizes the fact that the girls all belong to the same group.

7   As Joy and Tommy grow up, they will continue to speak differently. In junior high school, Joy's status will depend on her circle of friends. If her friends are popular, then Joy may enjoy high status at school. For this reason, Joy and many other girls are interested in gossip. If Joy has some information to share about a popular girl at school, this proves that she has a friendship with this girl. In this way Joy can use gossip to gain more status in her school.

8   Tommy, on the other hand, may be less interested in gossip. His status does not depend on who his friends are at school. Tommy gains status through his own ability to play sports well or earn high grades. Later in life, Joy may continue to be interested in talking about other people and their lives. Tommy will be less interested in personal talk and more concerned with discussions of sports and news. These give him a chance to gain status by showing others his knowledge.

9   Different ways of speaking are part of gender. As adults, men and women sometimes face difficulties in their communication with each other. Studies of communication show that if a woman tells her husband about a problem, she will expect him to listen and offer sympathy. She may be annoyed when he simply tells her how to solve the problem. Similarly, a husband may be annoyed when his wife wants to stop and ask a stranger for directions to a park or restaurant. Unlike his wife, he would rather use a map and find his way by himself.

10   Language is also part of the different ways that men and women think about friendship. Most North American men believe that friendship means doing things together such as camping or playing tennis. Talking is not an important part of friendship for most of them. American women, on the other hand, usually identify their best friend as someone with whom they talk frequently. Tannen believes that for women, talking with friends and agreeing with them is very important. Tannen has found that women, in contrast to men, often use tag questions. For example, a woman might say, "This is a great restaurant, isn't it?" By adding a tag question to her speech ("isn't it?"), she is giving other people a chance to agree with her. Likewise, many women use more polite forms—"Can you close the door?" "Could you help me?" "Would you come here?" Men, however, often speak more directly, giving direct commands—"Close the door." "Help me." "Come here."

11   These differences seem to be part of growing up in the culture of the United States and following its rules of gender. If men and women can understand that many of their differences are cultural, not personal, they may be able to improve their relationships. They may begin to understand that because of gender differences in language, there is more than one way to communicate.

Did the reading include the information you expected? Look back at your ideas on page 76.

READING FOR MAIN IDEAS

*Write **T** (true) or **F** (false) for each statement according to the reading. Rewrite the false statements to make them true.*

Gender

_____ **1.** A child's sex at birth determines how the child will think, act, and speak later in life.

_____ **2.** People learn masculine and feminine behavior.

_____ **3.** Men and women learn to use language differently.

_____ **4.** Gender differences can be seen in the ways that children use language when they fight.

_____ **5.** Differences in communication between males and females are the same in all cultures.

_____ **6.** Girls gain status by showing their knowledge about sports and news.

_____ **7.** Girls get much of their identity from being part of a group.

_____ **8.** Men usually talk more about other people than women do.

READING FOR DETAILS

Circle the best answer for each question. Write the number of the paragraph where you found the answer.

Paragraph

1. In what kind of group does Tommy like to play?   *2*
   a. He likes to play in groups of both boys and girls.
   b. He likes to play in large groups.
   c. He likes to play in small groups.

2. How did Joy's mother first show that Joy was a girl?   _____
   a. She put a pink hairband around her head.
   b. She put a pink dress on her.
   c. She painted her room blue.

3. What does Tommy like about being captain?   _____
   a. He likes boasting.
   b. He likes telling other boys what to do.
   c. He likes having the other boys like him.

4. How do boys get attention?   _____
   a. They argue with others.
   b. They talk about their abilities.
   c. They change the rules.

5. Who do girls usually play with?   _____
   a. They play with small groups of girls.
   b. They play with large groups of girls.
   c. They play with groups of both boys and girls.

6. What is one reason why girls are interested in gossip?   _____
   a. Gossip teaches them how to act.
   b. Gossip allows them to use commands.
   c. Gossip can bring them status.

7. Why might a woman get angry with her husband?   _____
   a. She feels that he doesn't listen.
   b. She feels that his advice is wrong.
   c. She feels that he doesn't care.

8. How do American men show friendship?   _____
   a. They show friendship by talking together often.
   b. They show friendship by agreeing with each other.
   c. They show friendship by doing things together.

REACTING TO THE READING

1 *Look at Reading One to help you answer the questions below. Circle your answer, and write the number of the paragraph where you found the information. Then discuss your answers. (More than one answer may be possible for some questions.)*

Paragraph

1. When do gender differences between boys and girls begin?   _____
   a. before birth
   b. at birth
   c. shortly after birth

2. Why were different colors used in the children's rooms?   _____
   a. for variety
   b. because of preference
   c. as a reflection of gender

3. What might Tommy do if he played with Joy and her friends?   _____
   a. argue with them
   b. tell them what to do
   c. invite other boys to join the group

4. Compared to Tommy's friendships, Joy's friendships are
   probably . . .   _____
   a. more boring.
   b. longer lasting.
   c. less competitive.

5. "Gender" refers to behavior that is considered masculine
   or feminine according to . . .   _____
   a. each person.
   b. members of a culture.
   c. family members.

6. Which of the following is emphasized in girls' speech?   _____
   a. belonging to a group
   b. playing fairly
   c. being liked

7. What do some men want to prove by discussing sports?   _____
   a. They are knowledgeable.
   b. They are masculine.
   c. They are interested in sports.

8. What do the differences in male and female language show?   _____
   a. Human relationships are difficult.
   b. Human communication is not simple.
   c. Humans can be divided into two genders.

2 *Discuss these questions with your classmates.*

1. Do you believe that men and women may have difficulties in their
   relationships just because of different styles of communication?

2. The author of "Different Ways of Talking" believes it is helpful for men and
   women to think about the language and culture of the opposite sex. Do you
   agree? Why or why not?

B   READING TWO: *Speaking of Gender*

1 *Read the following imaginary interview. Dr. Glib Speakwell is a professor of
communications at a well-known university. She is being interviewed by Gigi Jones,
a reporter for* Lingo *magazine.*

SPEAKING OF GENDER

By Gigi Jones (from *Lingo* magazine)

Gigi Jones (GJ): I know you've written a lot about gender and language, Dr. Speakwell.

Dr. Speakwell (DS): Yes, I have. I find it very interesting. For example, you just called me "Doctor." That used to always suggest a man, not a woman.

GJ: Maybe I should call you "Doctorette."

DS: Actually, I prefer to be called "Doctor."

GJ: Why is that?

DS: Well, you know, English has several feminine words that people sometimes use when they're referring to women. You probably know them, right? *Poetess, songstress, bachelorette?* Now these words aren't used too often, but they exist in the language. However, some women don't like such words because they feel as if these words make women less important than men.

GJ: What do you mean by that?

DS: For instance, if you say the word *actress,* people don't always think of a serious artist. They might think of some silly, beautiful female who's more worried about her makeup than she is about Shakespeare. But when you say *actor—* that's not silly at all. That's a serious word, a respectable word.

GJ: I see.

DS: That's why I would never call myself a doctorette. Or a professoress—never!

GJ: Fine. I'll call you doctor.

DS: And I'll call you Ms. Jones. That's a very good example of how the language has changed in recent years, partly as a result of the women's movement.

GJ: You mean the title of *Ms.?*

DS: Not just that. We've changed dozens of words related to occupations. Think of all the words that used to end in *-man. Policeman, fireman, mailman, . . .*

GJ: I guess they've all changed. Now we say *police officer, firefighter, . . .* but what about *mailman?*

DS: *Mail carrier.* And do you know why? We've removed gender from these words because, after all, both men and women can do these jobs.

GJ: I suppose. But not everyone would agree with you.

DS: Maybe not. But you know, even though I believe men and women are equal in their abilities, I do think there are differences in the way they speak.

GJ: Do you really think so?

DS: Absolutely. Look at all the color words that women know! If a man and woman go shopping together, the man will look at a shirt and say, *I like the purple one.* But a woman will look at the same shirt and call it *lavender . . .* or *periwinkle. . . .*

GJ: Or *mauve?*

DS: Right! Women use more words for color. They also use some adjectives that men don't use . . . such as *lovely, cute, adorable.*

GJ: I guess you're right. Most men don't seem to use those words.

DS: Most of them don't. But you know, language and gender are both so closely related to culture. In fact, I've studied seventeen countries, and I found out that in Japan, for example, men and women use different word endings. So if a man doesn't want to sound bossy, he'll use the feminine word ending, *-no,* instead of *-ka. Ka* sounds more masculine, more direct.

GJ: So a man will talk like a woman in certain situations. That's fascinating. Thank you.

DS: My pleasure.

2 *Discuss these questions with the class.*

1. Do you agree with Dr. Speakwell's idea that men and women speak differently? Give examples to support your opinion.

2. In English, there are three titles for women: *Miss, Mrs.,* and *Ms.* How are they different? Why do you think *Ms.* is used today? What titles are used in your native language for men or women?

3. How does your native language use words related to occupation? Do these words show gender differences? Explain.

C   LINKING READINGS ONE AND TWO

*Decide whether the following quotations are more usual for a male or female to say. Write **M** (male) or **F** (female) next to each quotation. Use the readings to help you decide. Then explain your answer to the class, using information from the readings.*

_____   1. "Let's try it again."

_____   2. "Don't throw it to him!"

_____   3. "Look at me. I can jump higher than you."

_____   4. "It's a beautiful day, isn't it?"

_____   5. "You're my best friend."

_____   6. "Did you see the game last night?"

_____   7. "Excuse me. Can you tell me where Chestnut Street is?"

_____   8. "What an adorable outfit you're wearing. Really cute."

_____   9. "I don't think they're going to win this year."

_____   10. "What a lovely gift! I really like that burgundy color."

3 Focus on Vocabulary

1 *In "Speaking of Gender" you learned about gender-specific words like* actor/actress *and* bachelor/bachelorette. *Categorize the occupations on page 84 as male, female, or unisex (a category for both genders). For some of the occupations, there may only be words for two categories.*

stewardess	server	seamstress	repair person
garment worker	host	salesman	waitress
sanitation worker	maid	flight attendant	repairman
waiter	salesperson	steward	hostess
butler	garbage man		

Male	Female	Unisex
	stewardess	

Now, work with a partner to brainstorm other gender-specific words in English. You may also want to include a few examples from your native language.

Male	Female	Unisex

2 *Look at the summary of Reading One below. Complete the sentences with words from the box. Make sure that each word fits the sentence grammatically. (You may need to change the form of the word to do this.) Use each word only once.*

feminine	masculine	emphasize	compete
fair	reflect	influence	gender
prove	status		

Boys and girls learn different ways of behaving, talking, and thinking. These different behaviors reflect differences in (1) _____ . In the American culture, boys learn to (2) _____ with each other in games, trying very hard to win and boasting about how well they can do things. These behaviors are considered (3) _____ . People expect boys to act in these ways. On the other hand, girls learn to be (4) _____ . They would rather have their friends like them than compete with them to win a game. Girls are more interested in being (5) _____ , or equal, when they play. As children grow up, their gender will (6) _____ their behavior. Language (7) _____ the gender of children. Boys usually give commands, while girls often make suggestions. When boys use commands, it (8) _____ their leadership. As they grow older, their (9) _____ in society will depend on different things. Boys will gain respect by their achievements in school and in sports, by their leadership, and by showing their knowledge. Girls will gain respect by having friends who are popular. Sharing gossip about a friend is one of the ways they (10) _____ their friendship.

3 *Imagine that you are a reporter. On a separate piece of paper, write three to four questions for Dr. Speakwell. In each question, use at least one of the vocabulary words from Exercises 1 and 2. Then share your questions with another student, and discuss possible answers.*

4 Focus on Writing

A STYLE: Comparing and Contrasting

1 *Read the following paragraphs taken from "Different Ways of Talking." Look at the underlined words. What do they mean?*

Different ways of speaking are part of gender. As adults, men and women sometimes face difficulties in their communication with each other. Studies of communication show that if a woman tells her husband about a problem, she will expect him to listen and offer sympathy. She may be annoyed when he simply tells her how to solve the problem. <u>Similarly</u>, a husband may be annoyed when his wife wants to stop and ask a stranger for directions to a park or restaurant. <u>Unlike</u> his wife, he would rather use a map and find his way by himself.

Language is <u>also</u> part of the different ways that men and women think about friendship. Most North American men believe that friendship means doing things together such as camping or playing tennis. Talking is not an important part of friendship for most of them. American women, <u>on the other hand</u>, usually identify their best friend as someone with whom they talk frequently. Tannen believes that for women, talking with friends and agreeing with them is very important.

Writers use **transitions** to help readers move from one idea to another. These words or phrases prepare the reader for what type of information will come next. A variety of transitions are used to compare, or show similarities, and to contrast, or show differences.

Transitions Used to Compare

similarly   *also*   *likewise*

- **Similarly,** a husband may be annoyed when his wife wants to stop and ask a stranger for directions to a park or restaurant.

- Language is **also** part of the different ways that men and women think about friendship.

- **Likewise,** many women use more polite forms—"Can you close the door?" "Could you help me?" "Would you come here?"

Transitions Used to Contrast

on the other hand   *however*   *unlike*   *in contrast to*

- **Unlike** his wife, he would rather use a map and find his way by himself.

- American women, **on the other hand,** usually identify their best friend as someone with whom they talk frequently.

- Tannen has found that women, **in contrast to** men, often use tag questions.

- Men, **however,** often speak more directly, giving direct commands—"Close the door." "Help me." "Come here."

---

2 *Rewrite the sentences on page 87 by adding the transition words in parentheses. You may need to combine some sentences and change the word order, too. For items 6 and 7, write your own sentences using information from "Speaking of Gender" and the words in parentheses. Then share them with the class.*

Example

Joy enjoyed helping her mother take care of the baby. She enjoyed playing with other girls at school. (also)

Joy enjoyed helping her mother take care of the baby. She also enjoyed playing with other girls at school.

1. Joy loves jumping rope with her two best friends. Tommy likes to play ball with a large group of boys. (in contrast to)

   _____

   _____

   _____

2. Tommy enjoys telling the other boys what to do. Joy doesn't like it when new girls join her friends. (on the other hand)

   _____

   _____

   _____

3. Boys might play in large groups in which every boy knows his place. Girls usually play in smaller groups. (however)

   _____

   _____

   _____

4. Boys compete with one another for leadership. Most girls want other girls to like them, and this is more important to them than winning. (unlike)

   _____

   _____

   _____

5. A woman may be annoyed when her husband simply tells her how to solve the problem. A husband may be annoyed when his wife wants to stop and ask a stranger for directions. (likewise)

   _____

   _____

   _____

6. (similarly) _____

   _____

   _____

7. (also) _____

   _____

   _____

B   GRAMMAR: Using Modals for Requests

1 *Read the following pairs of sentences, and circle the ones that seem more polite.*

1. **a.** Sign this form.

   b. Can you sign this form?

2. **a.** Could you help me?

   b. Help me.

3. **a.** Return my books.

   b. Would you return my books?

Modals for Requests

1. *Can, could,* and *would* are **modals.** They are often used to ask someone to do something. *Can* is used for informal requests. *Would* and *could* are used to soften requests and make them sound less demanding.

Can you help me?

Could you help me?

Would you help me?

2. We use *please* to make the request more polite.

Could you **please** help me?

3. A related form is *would you mind* + gerund. This is also a way to make polite requests.

Would you mind helping me?

2 *Below are sentences taken from "Different Ways of Talking" and questions about those situations. Write polite requests using modals.*

1. Joy loves jumping rope with her two best friends.

   How would she ask her friend to hand her the jump rope?

   Can *you hand me the rope* ?

2. If her friends are popular, then Joy may enjoy high status at school.

   How would Joy invite her friend to visit her house after school?

   Can _____ ?

3. Later in life, Joy may continue to be interested in talking about other people and their lives.

How would she ask her friend Ellen to tell her about her other friend Lisa?

Could _____ ?

4. Studies of communication show that if a woman tells her husband about a problem, she will expect him to listen and offer sympathy.

Mary wants to talk to her husband after dinner about a problem she's having. How would she ask him to come over to the sofa and listen to her problem?

Could _____ ?

5. A husband may be annoyed when his wife wants to stop and ask a stranger for directions to a park or restaurant.

How would she ask her husband to stop the car so she can ask for directions?

Would you mind _____ ?

3 *Write a polite request for each situation.*

1. You are writing an e-mail to ask for a catalogue from Baby Outfitters.

_____

_____

2. You want to ask the doctor for a copy of the sonogram image of your baby.

_____

_____

3. You are writing a letter to request that the hospital send you a new bill.

_____

_____

4. You are sending money to your local theater and asking for tickets for a play.

_____

_____

C WRITING TOPICS

Choose one of the following topics. Write two or three paragraphs using some of the vocabulary, grammar, and style you learned in this unit.

1. Are boys and girls treated differently in your home culture? Are they taught differently? Discuss similarities and differences in the ways boys and girls are treated.

2. Do you agree that men and women speak differently in your home culture? If you agree, explain the differences. Do men and women use different polite language? Do they ask for help in different ways? Do they use different word endings or beginnings? Is gossip used differently by men and women? What topics do men like to discuss with other men? What topics do women like to discuss with other women? Give examples.

3. Compare the status of men to the status of women in your home culture. How do men and women gain status?

4. Imagine a culture in which there are very few gender differences. Do you think life would be easier or more difficult? Give specific reasons.

D RESEARCH TOPIC

In this unit you learned about gender differences in the United States. These differences are often reflected in TV programs. Now you are going to investigate some TV programs for gender-specific language.

Step 1: Select a 30-minute drama or sitcom (situation comedy) program to watch. Listen for language and watch for behavior that you think is gender specific. You might find it helpful to videotape the program so that you can listen to it more than once. Complete the form on page 91.

1. Name of TV program:

2. Type of TV program:

3. List the main characters with a few words to describe each one.

4. Summarize the plot, or story, in one or two sentences.

5. List and identify any behaviors that you noticed were gender specific.

6. List any language that you noticed was gender specific.

Step 2:   Share what you learned with a small group of classmates. Was there any similarity or contrast in what your group found? Write a one-paragraph report summarizing your findings. If there is time, you may want to show a clip of the program you videotaped.

For step-by-step practice in the writing process, see *Writing Activity Book, Intermediate,* Unit 5.

Assignment	Comparison and Contrast Paragraphs
Prewriting	Making a Chart
Organizing	Comparing and Contrasting
Revising	Using Transitions of Comparison and Contrast
	Using Modals for Request
Editing	Punctuating Transitions of Comparison and Contrast

For Unit 5 Internet activities, visit the NorthStar Companion Website at http://www.longman.com/northstar.

Ecotourism

1 Focus on the Topic

A PREDICTING

Look at the map, and discuss these questions with the class.

1. Where is Antarctica?

2. What kind of people travel to Antarctica?

3. What would it be like to live there?

B SHARING INFORMATION

Work in groups of four. Discuss your past travel experiences. Share your group's answers with the class.

1. Describe a place that you have visited that had lots of natural beauty (trees, mountains, an ocean, and so on).

2. What wild animals have you seen in their natural environment?

3. What is the coldest place you have ever visited? How cold was it?

C PREPARING TO READ

BACKGROUND

Antarctica is one of the world's continents. How much do you know about this place? Circle the best answer to complete each sentence. Discuss your answers with the class. Then look at the answers at the bottom of the page.

1. About _____ of Antarctica's land is covered with ice.

   a. 25%   b. 50%   c. 75%   d. 98%

2. Antarctica is classified as _____.

   a. a desert   b. a rain forest   c. an ocean   d. a tundra

3. Antarctica is the _____ continent.

   a. coldest   b. windiest   c. driest   d. a, b, and c

4. Antarctica is the home of animals and birds, including the _____.

   a. eagle   b. bear   c. dodo   d. penguin

5. Most of the people in Antarctica are _____.

   a. skiers   b. scientists   c. tourists   d. Antarcticans

VOCABULARY FOR COMPREHENSION

*Guess what the underlined word means in each numbered sentence. Circle **T** (true) or **F** (false) for the statement that follows.*

1. The <u>tourists</u> were visiting three main cities during their travels in Italy: Rome, Florence, and Naples.

   T   F   The tourists were people who were working in Italy.

2. The desert <u>landscape</u> is very flat.

   T   F   "Landscape" means the way the land looks.

3. We must <u>preserve</u> the rain forest because it is the home of many birds that cannot live anywhere else.

   T   F   It would be good to cut down the rain forest now so we can use the wood.

4. The <u>ozone hole</u> may be dangerous to people who live on the earth. It is a hole in the ozone layer.

   T   F   The ozone layer is made of gases that protect the earth from the bad effects of the sun.

5. Some scientists believe that <u>global warming</u> will cause the ice of Antarctica to melt.

   T   F   The earth will become too hot.

6. That island is <u>inhabited</u> only by birds.

   T   F   All kinds of animals live there.

7. The highest mountain in the world is Mount Everest. I don't know how people can go there because it is such a <u>harsh</u> place.

   T   F   It's really quite comfortable.

8. Next summer I'm going to travel to a very <u>remote</u> part of Asia. It will take a long time to get there, but I want to go to a place where few visitors have gone.

   T   F   This is a place that's easy to get to from the big city.

9. His wife said, "Think about the <u>consequences</u> if you lose your job."

   T   F   She might want her husband to think about not having any money to pay the bills for the family.

10. The <u>coastal</u> cities of a country are often popular vacation spots because people like to be near the ocean.

   T   F   These places are often in the center of the country.

11. The oceans of the world are <u>vast</u> places of water.

    T   F   The oceans are smaller than other places of water.

12. The ice on the pond was so <u>fragile</u> that the children couldn't ice skate.

    T   F   The ice could break easily.

2 Focus on Reading

A   READING ONE: *Tourists in a Fragile Land*

You are going to read an opinion essay about tourism in Antarctica. The essay was written by a scientist who works there. What do you think his opinion will be? Choose one.

    a. Tourists should not visit Antarctica because they may cause problems.

    b. Tourists should visit Antarctica because there is so much for them to learn.

    c. Tourists to Antarctica should pay a special tax to help scientists with their work there.

TOURISTS IN A
FRAGILE LAND

1 As a scientist working in Antarctica, I spend most of my time in the lab studying ice. I am trying to find out the age of Antarctic ice. All we know for certain is that it is the oldest ice in the world. The more we understand it, the more we will understand the changing weather of the Earth. Today, as with an increasing number of days, I had to leave my work to greet a group of tourists who were taking a vacation in this continent of ice. And although I can appreciate their desire to experience this beautiful land-scape, I feel Antarctica should be closed to tourists.

2   Antarctica is the center of important scientific research, and it must be preserved for this purpose. Meteorologists are now looking at the effects of the ozone hole that was discovered above Antarctica in 1984. They are also trying to understand global warming. If the earth's temperature continues to increase, the health and safety of every living thing on the planet will be affected. Astronomers have a unique view of space and are able to see it very clearly from Antarctica. Biologists have a chance to learn more about the animals that inhabit the frozen land. Botanists study the plant life to understand how it can live in such a harsh environment, and geologists study the Earth to learn more about how it was formed. There are even psychologists who study how people behave when they live and work together in such a remote location.

3   When tourist groups come here, they take us away from our research. Our work is difficult, and some of our projects can be damaged by such simple mistakes as opening the wrong door or bumping into a small piece of equipment. In addition, tourists in Antarctica can also hurt the environment. Members of Greenpeace, one of the world's leading environmental organizations, complain that tourists leave trash on beaches and disturb the plants and animals. In a place as frozen as Antarctica, it can take 100 years for a plant to grow back, and tourists taking pictures of baby penguins may not pay close attention to what their feet are stepping on. Oil spills are another problem caused by tourism. In 1989, one cruise ship caused an oil spill that killed many penguins and destroyed a five-year scientific project.

4   The need to protect Antarctica from tourists becomes even greater when we consider the fact that there is no government here. Antarctica belongs to no country. Who is making sure that the penguins, plants, and sea are safe? No one is responsible. In fact, we scientists are only temporary visitors ourselves. It is true that the number of tourists who visit Antarctica each year is small compared to the number of those who visit other places. However, these other places are inhabited by local residents and controlled by local governments. They have an interest in protecting their natural environments. Who is concerned about the environment of Antarctica? The scientists, to be sure, but not necessarily the tour companies that make money from sending people south.

5   If we don't protect Antarctica from tourism, there may be serious consequences for us all. The ice of Antarctica holds 70 percent of the world's fresh water. If this ice melts, ocean levels could rise 200 feet and flood the coastal cities of the Earth. Also, the continent's vast fields of ice provide natural air conditioning for our planet. They keep the Earth from getting too hot as they reflect sunlight back into space. Clearly, Antarctica should remain a place for careful and controlled scientific research. We cannot allow tourism to bring possible danger to the planet. The only way to protect this fragile and important part of the planet is to stop tourists from traveling to Antarctica.

READING FOR MAIN IDEAS

1 *Look at the prediction you chose about Reading One on page 96. Was your prediction correct?*

2 *Number the following main ideas in the order they appear in Reading One.*

_____ Antarctica has no government.

_____ The entire world may be affected by problems in Antarctica.

_____ Many different scientists learn new things by studying Antarctica.

READING FOR DETAILS

1 *Complete the following outline with details from Reading One.*

I. Scientists learn new things in Antarctica because it is different from other places.

    a. _____ ice in the world

    b. Unique _____ of space

    c. Very _____ environment

II. Problems in Antarctica may affect the world.

    a. Large _____ above Antarctica

    b. Ice = _____ percent of the earth's fresh water

    c. _____ = Earth's air conditioner

2 *The following statements are false or incomplete. Rewrite them according to Reading One so that they are true and complete.*

1. The writer of the essay knows the age of Antarctic ice.

The writer of the essay is trying to find out the age of Antarctic ice.

2. The writer wants Antarctica to be closed.

_____

3. Psychologists study how people behave when they get lost in Antarctica.

_____

4. The oil spill caused by a cruise ship killed many scientists.

_____

5. Tour companies may be concerned about the environment of Antarctica.

_____

6. If we stop tourism in Antarctica, there may be consequences for tour companies.

_____

7. The ice of Antarctica attracts sunlight and heats the Earth.

_____

REACTING TO THE READING

1 _The scientist uses details to make his opinion essay more interesting. Read the details in the following statements. Circle the best answer to complete each statement._

1. The tourists enjoy Antarctica because of its _____.
   a. beautiful landscape   **b.** unique view of space

2. One problem with tourists who visit scientists is that they may _____.
   a. ask too many questions   **b.** do too much research

3. Another problem with tourists is that they may _____.
   a. leave trash on beaches   **b.** eat penguin eggs

4. The time that a scientist spends in Antarctica is always _____.
   a. difficult   **b.** limited

5. Other tourist places in the world are controlled by local people who want to _____.
   a. take care of their local environment   **b.** destroy natural beauty

6. If tourism continues in Antarctica, people who live near oceans may be affected by _____.
   a. bad weather   **b.** flooding

2 _Discuss these questions with a partner._

1. If you were a scientist in Antarctica, how would you feel about tourists? Explain.

2. Can you find any weakness in the writer's opinion? Do you agree with everything he says? How much do you agree with him?

B   READING TWO: *A Travel Journal*

1 *Read the following pages from the journal of a tourist who traveled to Antarctica.*

A Travel Journal

Chile, South America   **February 16**

The sunlight was shining so brightly as our plane flew over the snow-covered Andes mountains, which seem to go on forever.

Island of Cape Horn   **February 18**

We spent the morning at a small church named Star of the Sea. This is a quiet place where visitors are invited to remember all the international sailors who died here. They were all trying to sail around the southern point of South America, and many of them lost their lives at sea.

Drake Passage—aboard the tour ship Explorer   **February 19**

We were welcomed today by the captain and crew. They gave us warm Antarctic jackets and introduced themselves to us. Sea birds followed the ship closely, sailing in the cold wind. As we headed south, we saw a pink ship in the distance. Our captain explained that it was not a ship but an iceberg[1]—the first one of our trip.

Deception Island, Antarctica   **February 21**

We landed on Bailey Head, where thousands and thousands of penguins greeted us. The crew gave us a set of rules to follow to protect the environment. Mark, one of the scientists on our ship, asked us to bring him any trash that we find. He is studying the amount of trash created by tourists in Antarctica each year.

Tonight we'll listen to Christina, another scientist. She will explain the plant and animal life to us. Then she will show us a video.

The more I see, the more I want to learn.

---

[1] *iceberg:* a large piece of ice in the ocean

Cuverville Island, Antarctica   February 23

We awakened this morning to the noisy sound of penguins. They're loud! We met a team of biologists living in tents. They are studying the effect of tourists on baby penguins. When our captain invited the biologists to come on board for a hot shower, they joined us immediately. Then we cruised through the icebergs, which appeared in unbelievable shapes and sizes, as the sun was sinking in the sky. They seemed to be works of art by an ice sculptor.[2]

Paradise Bay, Antarctica   February 25

Today we reached the mainland of the continent. Our guide today was Stephanie, who helped us walk through snow to a point about 500 feet above sea level. We were laughing like children when we reached the top—it was so much fun to be up there. Later, we explored the glaciers[3] in motorized rafts. The ice was as thick as the crushed ice in a soft drink, and as we pushed through it, the snow fell down like white flowers.

Detaille Island, Antarctica   February 28

We were drinking champagne to celebrate today while we were crossing the Antarctic Circle. Each year, only 300 visitors come this far south. Mark explained that the ice is blue down here because it catches all the colors of the rainbow except for blue. I have always thought of Antarctica as nothing but white. But now I see a clear blue light shining through the mountains of ice all around us, and I have no words to describe the beauty.

Our ship passed a huge field of frozen sea. Mark invited us to come out and play. We weren't sure at first, but when we felt how solid it was, we jumped and ran. All around us were mountains and glaciers that no one has ever explored. It amazed me to think that no human hand or foot has ever touched them; only a few human eyes have seen them.

When I get home, it will be hard for me to explain what this feeling of amazement was like, but I will try.

We all felt sad today when we realized that our ship was heading north. We really don't want to leave Antarctica, a unique world.

---

[2] *sculptor:* an artist who works with hard material such as marble or stone
[3] *glaciers:* mountains of ice

2 *Discuss the following questions with the class.*

- What kind of person do you think this tourist is?

- Do you think she did anything that was dangerous to Antarctica? Explain.

- Which part of her trip did she seem to enjoy the most? Which part would you enjoy the most? Explain.

- What did people on this trip do to protect Antarctica and keep it clean?

C   LINKING READINGS ONE AND TWO

1 *The chart below compares the views of the scientist with the views of the tourist. Look back at Readings One and Two, and fill in the missing information.*

OPINIONS OF THE SCIENTIST	OPINIONS OF THE TOURIST
1. The Antarctic environment must be preserved for research.	**1.** *As tourists learn about Antarctica and return home to tell their friends and families about its importance, they may want to help preserve the environment of Antarctica.*
2. We cannot control the behavior of tourists.	**2.**
3.	**3.** Tourists can actually help scientists with their experiments.
4. Tourists don't care about Antarctica.	**4.**

2 *Which opinion do you agree with more—the scientist's or the tourist's? Why? Write your answer on a separate piece of paper. Then share it with the class.*

3 Focus on Vocabulary

1 *Match the adjectives in the box with the nouns surrounding them from Readings One and Two. Work with a partner to list as many possible combinations as you can think of on a separate piece of paper.*

Example: *unique landscape*

tourism   ozone hole

effect   oil spill

Adjectives

sea birds   unique   fragile   landscape

coastal   frozen

temperature   remote   scientific   consequences

research   harsh   natural   continent

vast   oldest

ice   tourists

global warming   weather

2 *Read the list of analogy types, their definitions, and the examples. Then analyze the relationships among the vocabulary words from the text. Circle the word that best completes each analogy. Be sure that the second pair of words has a similar relationship to the first pair of words. Label each with the analogy type.*

Analogy Types	Definitions	Examples
Synonym (**S**)	The words have the same meaning.	work : job
Antonym (**A**)	The words have the opposite meaning.	harsh : gentle
Cause/effect (**C/E**)	One word or phrase is the result of another word or phrase.	oil spill : death of penguins
Degree (**D**)	One word has a stronger meaning than the other.	damaged : destroyed
User/tool (**U**)	One word describes a person, and the other word describes the tool used by the person.	scientist : microscope
Necessity (**N**)	One word is needed for the other word to function.	water : shower

_S_   1. unique : rare = huge : _____

      a. fragile   **b.** remote   (**c.** vast)

_____   2. heavy rain : flood = vast ice fields : _____

      a. cool weather   **b.** ozone layer   **c.** lightning

_____   3. protected : preserved = worried : _____

      a. happy   **b.** concerned   **c.** careful

_____   4. harsh : comfortable = inland : _____

      a. coastal   **b.** mountain   **c.** ocean

_____   5. swimming : water = research : _____

      a. paper   **b.** books   **c.** facts

_____   6. traveler : map = astronomer : _____

      a. microscope   **b.** telescope   **c.** equipment

_____   7. old : ancient = far : _____

      a. young   **b.** remote   **c.** near

_____   8. increase : decrease = delicate : _____

      a. harsh   **b.** fragile   **c.** strong

_____   9. problem : crisis = knowledge : _____

      a. expertise   **b.** information   **c.** worry

_____   10. consequence : result = traveler : _____

      a. tourist   **b.** guide   **c.** researcher

3 *Write a question to go with each answer. Use the words in parentheses in your questions. You may need to change some word forms.*

  1. ANSWER: Nobody lives in Antarctica permanently. (inhabitants)

     QUESTION: _Are there any inhabitants who live in Antarctica all year?_

  2. ANSWER: Antarctica is a center of important scientific research. (preserve)

     QUESTION: _____

  3. ANSWER: Tourist groups interrupt or ruin scientific research, harm the environment, and can even increase the likelihood of oil spills by bringing cruise ships down there. (tourism)

     QUESTION: _____

4. ANSWER: They provide natural air conditioning for our planet. (vast)

   QUESTION: _____

5. ANSWER: It is made of gases that protect the earth from the bad effects of the sun. (ozone layer)

   QUESTION: _____

6. ANSWER: The ice could melt so that ocean levels would rise and flood the coastal cities of the Earth. (consequence)

   QUESTION: _____

7. Answer: We can do it by stopping tourists from going there. (fragile)

   QUESTION: _____

8. ANSWER: Some people worry that Antarctica will not be protected because it has no government. (concerned about)

   QUESTION: _____

4 Focus on Writing

A STYLE: Writing an Opinion Essay

1 *"Tourists in a Fragile Land" is an opinion essay. How is an opinion essay different from other types of writing you have done? How is it organized? What do you think makes an opinion essay effective?*

An essay is a piece of writing that has more than one or two paragraphs and is organized in a specific way. An **opinion essay** expresses an opinion about something. There are three important parts of a good opinion essay:

1. **The introductory paragraph** introduces the topic by giving general statements. These statements catch the reader's attention. They may tell about the importance of the subject or give background information. The last sentence of the paragraph contains the thesis statement. The thesis statement is like the topic sentence of a paragraph. It gives the specific topic and the main idea of the essay. In an opinion essay, it states the writer's opinion about the topic.

(continued)

> **2. The body** is the part of the essay that explains or supports the main idea in the thesis statement. The writer gives reasons, examples, explanations, and facts to show why he or she believes something. It can be one paragraph, but it is usually more than one. Each paragraph of the body has a topic sentence and supporting details.
>
> **3. The concluding paragraph** restates the main idea of the thesis statement. It can also contain a summary of the supporting details in the body, make a prediction about the future, or make suggestions for the future.

2 *Refer to "Tourists in a Fragile Land" to complete the following tasks.*

The Introduction

1. Find the thesis statement. Copy it here.

_____

2. Write a summary sentence of the information in the rest of the introduction. (the first paragraph)

_____

_____

The Body

3. Underline the topic sentence of each of the remaining paragraphs.

4. In paragraph 3, what type of supporting details are used? (reason, example, explanation, or fact)

_____

5. In paragraph 4, what type of supporting details are used?

_____

The Conclusion

6. Find the concluding sentence that restates the main idea. Write it here.

_____

_____

7. Does the concluding paragraph summarize the supporting details in the body? Does it make a prediction about the future? Does it make a suggestion for the future?

_____

_____

3 *Now that you've analyzed the essay in Reading One, imagine you're a tourist who wants Antarctica to be open to tourism and you're writing an opinion essay. Go back to Section 2C, Linking Readings One and Two (page 102), and use the tourist's points to develop one or two paragraphs for the body of the essay below.*

As a tourist who has been to Antarctica, I can tell you that it is a life-changing experience. I remember watching the clear, blue light shining through the mountains of ice all around us. It was amazing. I also remember how we were laughing like children when we reached the top of a snowy point 500 feet above sea level. I will never forget the beauty that I saw, the things that I learned, and the experience of being in a place where so few humans have been. Now I understand the importance of respecting our fragile planet. I know that some people want to make it impossible for tourists to visit this amazing continent, but I still believe every person should have the opportunity to go to Antarctica and see what I have seen.

There are so many reasons why Antarctica should be visited by tourists.

If tourists are not allowed to visit Antarctica, they will never experience how important it is. They will never understand how fragile the environment there is. They will never feel curious about how things grow in such a cold place. They will never stare in awe at the unspeakable beauty of blue ice mountains. And they will never return home to teach their friends and family what they've learned. Antarctica must be left open so that tourists can experience all it has to offer and know its value.

B   GRAMMAR: Past Progressive and Simple Past

1 *Read these sentences based on "A Travel Journal." Look at the underlined verbs. What is the difference between the verb forms in the sentences? Notice the boldfaced words. How are the meanings of* **when** *and* **while** *different?*

- We <u>were laughing</u> like children **when** we <u>reached</u> the top of a snowy point 500 feet above sea level.

- The sunlight <u>was shining</u> so brightly **when** our plane <u>flew</u> over the Andes mountains.

- We <u>were drinking</u> champagne **while** we <u>were crossing</u> the Antarctic Circle.

Past Progressive and Simple Past

1. Use the **simple past tense** to talk about actions, states, and situations in the past that are finished. The simple past tense of regular verbs is formed by adding **-d** or **-ed** to the base form of the verb.	Sea birds **followed** the ship closely.
2. Use the **past progressive,** also called **past continuous,** to describe a continuous nonstop action that was in progress at a specific time in the past. Examples of specific time include: *yesterday, last night, at that time.* The past progressive is formed like this: **be (past) + verb + -ing.**	The sunlight **was shining** so brightly on the glaciers.
3. Use the **past progressive** with the **simple past tense** to talk about an action that was interrupted by another action. Use the simple past tense for the interrupting action. Use **when** to introduce the simple past tense action.	We **were laughing** like children **when** we **reached** the top.
4. If you put the **when** clause first, you must put a comma at the end of the clause.	**When** we **reached** the top**,** we **were laughing** like children.
5. Use the **past progressive** with **while** to describe two actions in progress at the same time in the past.	We **were drinking** champagne **while** we **were crossing** the Antarctic Circle.
The **simple past** can also be used in the **while** clause without changing the meaning.	We were drinking champagne while we **crossed** the Antarctic Circle.

2 *Complete the sentences below with the words in parentheses. Use the **simple past** or **past progressive.** Write the new sentence on the line.*

1. Mark was studying the amount of trash created by tourists in Antarctica when . . .

   (he/become sick)

   Mark was studying the amount of trash created by tourists in Antarctica

   when he became sick.

2. The biologists were taking showers while . . .

   (we/eat/lunch)

   _____

   _____

3. I cried when . . .

   (I/get off/the boat)

   _____

   _____

4. Many sailors lost their lives while . . .

   (they/try to sail around South America)

   _____

   _____

5. We were running and jumping on the iceberg when . . .

   (it/start/to break)

   _____

   _____

6. The tourists arrived while the scientist . . .

   (work on an experiment)

   _____

   _____

3 *Think about the last time you took a vacation or the last time you went somewhere in a group. What were you doing? What were other people doing? On a separate piece of paper, write two sentences with **while** and two sentences with **when.***

C WRITING TOPICS

Choose one of the following topics. Write an opinion essay using some of the vocabulary and grammar that you learned in this unit.

1. Do you believe Antarctica should be closed to tourists? Why or why not?

2. Can you think of any places in the world that should be closed to tourists? Why? Explain.

3. In your opinion, which remote place is the best one for tourists to visit? Why?

4. Is it possible for scientists and tourists to work together to protect the environment? Explain.

5. Describe a place you know that has been helped (or hurt) by tourism. Give details.

6. How can tour companies help to make sure that the environment in Antarctica is safe?

D RESEARCH TOPIC

Find out about a controversial tourist destination. Below are some suggested places:

Antarctica	The Arctic (North Pole)	Costa Rica
The Amazon rain forest	Thailand	Peru

Step 1: Pick a fragile environment. Go to a travel agency to get information about it.

Step 2: Use the Internet or library to find the name of a local, national, or international organization that is working to protect this environment. Write to this organization, and ask these questions.

- Are there any accidents that have happened because of tourists in this place?

- How do the local people respond to tourism? Are they happy to have tourists? Are they harmed by the presence of tourists?

- Is the ecosystem* of this place endangered in any way because of the presence of tourists?

- How has the local environment been changed by the presence of tourists?

---

ecosystem: a community of organisms and their environment

Now add three questions of your own:

- _____
  _____

- _____
  _____

- _____
  _____

Step 3:   When you get an answer, share the letter with your class.

For step-by-step practice in the writing process, see *Writing Activity Book, Intermediate,* Unit 6.

Assignment	Opinion Essay
Prewriting	Listing
Organizing	Writing an Opinion Essay
Revising	Choosing Effective Supporting Details
	Using the Past Progressive and Simple Past Tense
Editing	Punctuating Sentences with *When* and *While*

For Unit 6 Internet activities, visit the NorthStar Companion Website at
http://www.longman.com/northstar.

What's So Funny about That?

1 Focus on the Topic

A PREDICTING

The photo above shows a scene from *I Love Lucy*, a famous TV show from the 1950s. Work with a partner to write a caption for the photo. Then share your caption with the class.

113

B   SHARING INFORMATION

People all over the world like to tell jokes or stories. One type of joke in the United States is called a **knock-knock joke.** It's a joke that begins with "Knock, Knock" and ends with a double meaning.

> **Example**
>
> A: Knock, knock.
>
> B: Who's there?
>
> A: Boo.
>
> B: Boo who?
>
> A: Why are you crying?

This joke is funny because "boo who" sounds like "boo hoo," a sound that people make when they are crying. Another type of joke that uses a double meaning is called a **pun.**

> **Example**
>
> A: What did the big strawberry say to the little strawberry?
>
> B: I don't know.
>
> A: If you weren't so sweet, we wouldn't be in this jam!

This joke uses the double meaning of "jam." It means "preserved fruit" and also means "being in a difficult situation."

1 *Ask three students these questions.*

1. Do you tell jokes?

2. Do you usually understand jokes in English? Why or why not?

3. Can you tell a joke in English? If so, tell it.

2 *Discuss with the class.*

1. Which joke was the funniest?

2. What made it funny?

C   PREPARING TO READ

BACKGROUND

Read the following paragraphs about I Love Lucy.

I Love Lucy was a popular American TV show during the 1950s. It was created by a married couple, Desi Arnaz and Lucille Ball. It was the first television show with a live audience.* The star of this show was a housewife named Lucy Ricardo. She was always doing funny things and getting into trouble. Lucy's type of comedy, based on funny physical movements, is called "slapstick."

Lucy's husband, Ricky Ricardo, was an immigrant from Cuba who spoke English with an accent. At times, he got angry or excited and spoke Spanish on the show. *I Love Lucy* became the highest-rated show in North America, and people still watch it on cable television today. It seems that people who enjoy comedy will always love Lucy.

Based on the paragraphs above, predict which of the statements you will find out more about in Reading One. Mark the statement(s) with a check (✓).

_____ **a.** The actors and actresses on the TV show did a lot of funny stunts.

_____ **b.** Even though Lucy Ricardo was a housewife, she wanted to be a star.

_____ **c.** The other main characters on the show were a married couple who were the friends of Lucy and Ricky.

_____ **d.** Ricky Ricardo worked as a computer programmer.

_____ **e.** The humor on the show was sometimes mean.

---

* *live audience:* an audience in the TV studio

VOCABULARY FOR COMPREHENSION

A TV producer works with actors, writers, and directors to plan a TV show. The passages below describe a meeting of TV producers who want to create a new comedy show. Match the underlined words in the passages with the definitions below.

Many actors have an <u>ambition</u> to be on television, and this new show will
(1)
give a few of them an <u>opportunity</u> to make their dreams come true. On this
(2)
show, some <u>scenes</u> will be humorous, and other parts will be filled with a
(3)
<u>tension</u> that makes the audience wonder what will happen next. The producers
(4)
believe that laughing at the tension on the show will help the audience <u>deal with</u>
(5)
their own tensions in life.

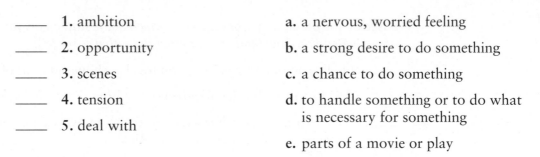

_____ **1.** ambition	**a.** a nervous, worried feeling
_____ **2.** opportunity	**b.** a strong desire to do something
_____ **3.** scenes	**c.** a chance to do something
_____ **4.** tension	**d.** to handle something or to do what is necessary for something
_____ **5.** deal with	**e.** parts of a movie or play

The star of the show will be a man who doesn't have a job outside of the home. His name will be Bob, and he will be married to a doctor. Bob will stay at home and take care of the children, clean the house, and cook all of the meals. His wife, Allison, will work long hours. But Bob will not see his life as <u>limited</u> in
(6)
any way, and he will not lose his <u>dignity</u> in this role; instead, he will be a full
(7)
partner with his wife, and it will be clear that she respects his mind and his abilities. And, although they will be married with kids, they will still <u>flirt with</u>
(8)
each other like newlyweds.

Another main character on the show will be Allison's father. He will always
<u>bicker</u> with his son-in-law because he won't understand why Bob stays at home
(9)

while Allison works to support the family. There will be tension between his
traditional ideas and Bob and Allison's modern ideas. Allison's mother will be
the kind of person who talks constantly but never listens. The producers have
decided that she will fall down a lot because she won't look where she is going.
The <u>stunts</u> she will do will add slapstick comedy to the show. She will also have
₍₁₀₎
a cute little dog, but this dog will be <u>mean</u>—always biting people for no reason.
₍₁₁₎

  The producers believe that the audience will like this show. They have already
shown scenes of it to a test audience, and the response was encouraging.

_____ 6. limited

_____ 7. dignity

_____ 8. flirt with

_____ 9. bicker

_____ 10. stunts

_____ 11. mean

f. argue

g. not nice; hurting someone or something
 with words or actions

h. self-respect

i. not having a lot of something

j. show romantic interest in

k. foolish or dangerous actions someone
 does to get attention

2 Focus on Reading

A READING ONE: *The Story of* I Love Lucy

*You are going to read a summary of the autobiography of Lucille Ball, the actress who
created* I Love Lucy *with her husband, Desi Arnaz. When people write about their true
experiences in life, they are writing autobiographies.*

*Look at the photo on page 113. What kind of experiences do you think Lucille Ball and
Desi Arnaz had while they were making their show? Discuss your ideas with a partner.*

Now, read the summary that follows.

THE STORY OF
I LOVE LUCY

1 My dream of being a TV star had finally come true. One day CBS studios told my husband, Desi, that they wanted to make a TV show about a funny married couple. We couldn't believe it. It was a very busy time for us—we were expecting the birth of our first child—and now we had the opportunity to create our own TV show. Desi and I were so confused about what to do. We were radio performers. At that time, TV was still something new, and most Hollywood stars were afraid of it. I knew that if our TV show failed, we might never work in the movies again. But this was also the first chance that Desi and I had to work together, and this was exactly what we wanted to do.

2 Our decision to create *I Love Lucy* was made. We thought of the characters for the show: Ricky and Lucy Ricardo. Ricky was a Cuban immigrant who worked as a bandleader in a New York night club. Lucy was his wife, a 1950s housewife with a crazy ambition to be in show business—just like her husband.

3 Desi clearly described and carefully summarized what his ideas for the show were. He told CBS that the show's humor would never be mean or unkind. Ricky and Lucy would be very much in love with each other and would never flirt with other characters. Most of all, Ricky would always keep his dignity as a man. He told the writers not to let Lucy surprise him. "If Lucy's going to play a trick on me, make it clear to the audience that Ricky knows what's going on." It was important to him to be seen as a strong male figure.

4 After we started making the show, I looked more and more like an expectant mother. During one of the first shows, I covered myself up with a funny costume: baggy clown pants that I wore while I played the cello. But no matter what I wore, I always played Lucy Ricardo as very feminine. I made sure that Lucy always looked soft and pretty, even when someone had thrown a pie in her face. And Lucy was never mean. When she got in trouble, it was usually because she was trying to be a star. I believe this is one reason why the audience liked the show. People in the audience could understand Lucy—because, really, who doesn't want to be a star?

5 Lucy's dream of being a star was one reason why *I Love Lucy* was a hit. Fred and Ethel were another reason. These characters were the neighbors of Ricky and Lucy, an older couple who were always bickering with each other. Ethel was played by Vivian Vance, an experienced

stage actress who didn't mind looking a bit plain. She agreed not to wear false eyelashes or eye makeup. But she refused to wear body padding to look heavier. She wanted to appear as a woman of average weight—not overweight—so that when her husband told her she was fat, the audience would see this as funny, not sad.

6   Fred was a henpecked husband[1] that so many men in the audience could understand. They loved it when Fred fought back with sharp words of his own. When people saw Bill Frawley, the actor who played Fred, on the street, they would often say, "Hey, Fred, you really know how to handle that wife of yours!" I believe the audience understood the husband-wife tension on the show. Maybe laughing about it helped them deal with their own tensions in life. As an actress, I worked hard to make the audience believe that Lucy was always a little afraid of Ricky. Of course, Lucy knew that Ricky loved her and was a good husband, but she also knew how limited his patience was. I think this tension between feeling loved and feeling afraid made the show more exciting and funnier to watch.

7   When people think of *I Love Lucy,* the slapstick comedy is usually what they remember. The only way I can do crazy stunts is to believe they are real. It's almost like becoming a child again. Only a child can really do a good job of pretending to eat like a dog under a table or pretending to freeze under burning stage lights. In one of the most famous scenes, Lucy and Ethel get a job in a chocolate factory. They have to wrap chocolates with paper, and the chocolates start coming out of the chocolate machine so fast that Lucy and Ethel have to start eating them. People always seem to remember that one.

8   But real life is not always comedy. After we found success with *I Love Lucy,* our marriage began to fall apart. The pressures of show business were destroying us as a couple. Desi and I finally reached the point where we were no longer speaking to each other. Of course, we continued to play the Ricky and Lucy characters as happily as usual.

9   We made our last show after we had agreed to divorce. During that show, Lucy was trying to find a way to help Ricky play his music on a famous and important TV show. She was dressed as a male chauffeur[2] with a cap and moustache. The humorous part of the scene was when Ricky pulled her close and kissed her, moustache and all. Maybe it seemed funny to the audience, but in reality, when we came eye-to-eye and really looked at each other, both of us started to cry.

---

[1] *henpecked husband:* a man who is always being told what to do by his wife
[2] *chauffeur:* someone whose job is to drive a car for another person

READING FOR MAIN IDEAS

*Write **T** (true) or **F** (false) for each statement according to the reading. Write which paragraph your information came from. Then change the false statements to true ones.*

Paragraph

_____ 1. Lucille Ball wanted both a baby and a TV show.   _____

_____ 2. Desi Arnaz was confused about his ideas for the show.   _____

_____ 3. The character of Lucy Ricardo wanted to be a housewife.   _____

_____ 4. Slapstick comedy is one reason why *I Love Lucy* is famous.   _____

_____ 5. Having a successful TV show did not help Lucille Ball's marriage.   _____

_____ 6. The tension between husband and wife in the show was one reason for the show's success.   _____

READING FOR DETAILS

The sentences below show how the information in the reading is organized. Read each sentence, and cross out one detail that is not included in the reading.

1. Before making *I Love Lucy*, Lucille Ball was _____.
   a. a wife
   b. an expectant mother
   c. an employee of CBS studios
   d. a radio performer

2. In the show *I Love Lucy*, _____.
   a. Lucy played tricks on Ricky
   b. Ricky kept his dignity
   c. Lucy surprised Ricky
   d. Ricky and Lucy loved each other

3. In the show, Lucy _____.
   a. was never mean
   b. dressed like a model
   c. was always feminine
   d. covered up the fact that she was going to have a baby

4. The relationship between Fred and Ethel included _____.
   a. arguments
   b. flirting with each other
   c. comments about weight
   d. criticism

5. Some examples of slapstick comedy in the show are _____.
   a. Lucy bakes a ten-foot loaf of bread
   b. Lucy pretends to eat like a dog
   c. Lucy and Ethel start eating chocolates because they can't wrap them fast enough
   d. Lucy has a pie thrown in her face

6. Toward the end of the life of the show _____.
   a. Lucy and Desi continued to play Ricky and Lucy as happily as usual
   b. Lucy and Desi really enjoyed their success
   c. Lucy and Desi weren't speaking to each other
   d. Lucy and Desi agreed to divorce

REACTING TO THE READING

1 *Look back at the ideas you predicted in Sections 1C (p. 115) and 2A (p. 117). Which ideas did you predict correctly? Discuss your predictions with the class.*

2 *Lucille Ball was an actress who created the character of Lucy Ricardo. Read the statements below. Check (✓) the statements that describe Lucille Ball and the ones that describe Lucy Ricardo. Some statements might describe both. Then discuss your answers with the class.*

	LUCILLE BALL	LUCY RICARDO
1. She had a busy career.	❏	❏
2. She dreamed of being in show business.	❏	❏
3. She stayed at home and took care of her family.	❏	❏
4. She knew how to play like a child.	❏	❏
5. She always looked soft and pretty.	❏	❏
6. She looked like an expectant mother.	❏	❏
7. She knew that her husband loved her even though she was a little bit afraid of him.	❏	❏

3 *I Love Lucy was successful because of slapstick comedy. It was also successful because people in the audience could understand the problems facing the characters in the show. Answer the questions. Then discuss your answers with your classmates.*

1. What are two examples of husband-wife tension in the show?

2. In the 1950s, the roles of men and women were different from what they are today. Describe the roles of Ricky and Lucy on the TV show. How might they be different today?

B   READING TWO: *Cosby: A Different Kind of Family Show*

1 *There are many types of comedy shows. I Love Lucy was one kind of humor. In the 1980s, Bill Cosby, a famous comedian, had a TV comedy show. It was very different from the* I Love Lucy *show. Read a review of* The Cosby Show.

Cosby: A Different Kind of Family Show

By Timothy Sargent (from the *Huntington Beach Herald*)

1   Heathcliff Huxtable. That's the name of Bill Cosby's TV character on *The Cosby Show*. Actually, he uses "Cliff" as a first name with family and friends. To the rest of the world he is "Dr. Huxtable," a kind and friendly obstetrician[1] married to a successful lawyer, Clair.

2   Cliff and Clair Huxtable. They are the loving African-American parents of five children: four girls and a boy. They live in a nice big house filled with pretty furniture. They are well dressed, and their children, ranging in age from preschool to high school, are bright and charming. Grandma and Grandpa are part of the fun, too. What's so funny about that? No pies are thrown; no funny costumes are worn. Instead, Dr. Huxtable relaxes at home in a

---

[1] *obstetrician:* a doctor who deals with the birth of children

sweater and does simple fatherly things. The children often bicker and make up, and sometimes there is tension between husband and wife. In the end Cliff and Clair look at each other, and we know what they are thinking: You're a pain in the neck, but I still love you.

3   Again, what's so funny about that? It's quite simple. Cliff and Clair show us family life in America not as it is, but as it could be. In a perfect world, both husband and wife have satisfying, high-paid careers. They still have time and energy to love their kids, and when pressures build up, they are able to laugh. Bill Cosby is the master of the chuckle.[2] He is able to do amazingly funny things with his face. When he raises his eyebrows, smiles, and chuckles, we know that everything is going to be all right—and this is comforting to all of us in the real world. Dr. Huxtable is here to show us that yes, life is a little frustrating at times, but if we chuckle our way through our problems and if we love the people around us, things are going to be OK.

4   In one show, Cliff has a cold but doesn't want to admit it to himself or anyone else. Every time someone asks him if he's sick, he denies it crossly.[3] Finally, at the end of the show, he admits it, and, like a child, asks his wife to take care of him: "I'm sick. Will you take care of me?" As Clair helps him climb the stairs she responds, "Yes."

Cliff continues with a series of questions like "Will you put me in the bed? Will you take my temperature? Will you make soup for me?" Clair says "Yes" each time. Finally, like a child who tries to use the situation to his advantage, Cliff asks "Will you buy me a pony?" We identify with Cliff's imperfections and are comforted to see that someone loves him anyway.

5   This is good medicine for America. What America needs to see right now is a happy family. Henry Louis Gates Jr., a professor of African-American studies at Harvard, tells us that Bill Cosby is a very smart man. Instead of focusing on the very real problems of race and money, he shows us "a black family dealing with all the things black people deal with, the same as all other people." For example, Theo, the teenage son, has been borrowing money from all his sisters. They finally tell him he needs to pay them back. NOW! But Theo has a problem. He doesn't have any money to pay them back with. So he asks his father for an advance on his allowance. Cliff says, "Son, you're already backed up to your 50th birthday. No." This is a familiar problem for many American families, but Cliff uses the humor of exaggeration to get his point across.

6   *The Cosby Show* is sure to please many people. I predict that the Huxtables will be in our lives for several years to come.

---

[2] *chuckle:* a quiet laugh
[3] *crossly:* in an annoyed manner

2 *Write answers for the following items. Then discuss them with a classmate.*

1. Describe the Huxtable family.

_____

_____

_____

_____

2. In your own words, explain why *The Cosby Show* is such a great success.

_____

_____

_____

_____

C   LINKING READINGS ONE AND TWO

1 *Now, compare* The Cosby Show *with your ideas about the* I Love Lucy *show. Write your answers, and discuss them with the class.*

1. In the 1950s, the roles of men and women were different from what they were in the 1980s. What differences can you find between the roles of Ricky and Cliff? Lucy and Clair?

_____

_____

_____

_____

_____

_____

_____

_____

2. Look at Reading One and Reading Two again. Label examples of humor that would be funny in your culture and that wouldn't be funny in your culture. Write funny or not funny next to the examples in the text. Can you explain why?

_____

_____

_____

_____

_____

_____

_____

2 *Lucille Ball died in 1989.* **The Cosby Show** *premiered in 1984. This means that Lucille Ball probably had a chance to watch* The Cosby Show. *Imagine that she is writing an article for a magazine comparing the two shows. Use information from both readings to complete the article.*

Times Have Changed

People often ask me what I like to watch on TV. I enjoy comedy, of course, and I think Bill Cosby's latest show is a lot of fun. I really like to see how the three different generations of Huxtables all get along. *The Cosby Show* also makes me think about how our society has changed along with our sense of humor. One of the biggest changes that I can think of is the role of women. When I played Lucy Ricardo, women _____.
Now we have the Cosby wife as an example of a woman who _____

_____.

In some ways, it seems like the 1980s have been a more difficult time for America than the 1950s were. Life seems more complicated now. I think people enjoyed *I Love Lucy* because it was so silly. On the other hand, *The Cosby Show* gives people a chance to see a family that _____.
I think it is important now when we can be so divided by differences of

_____.

I don't know if my first husband, Desi Arnaz, ever had a chance to see *The Cosby Show*. Sometimes I wonder what he would think of it. I know he enjoyed slapstick, so he might think *The Cosby Show* _____.
One thing I know he would like is how *The Cosby Show* _____

_____.

Life goes on, and everything changes. Television is a reflection of how we have changed. But I think one thing always stays the same: the power of humor to make us feel good. That's why TV stars may come and go, but TV comedy will always make us chuckle.

3 Focus on Vocabulary

1 *A* **suffix** *is a word ending that can change both the form of a word and its part of speech. For example, changing the adjective* **tense** *to* **tension** *makes it a noun. Look at the list of words below from Readings One and Two. Place them in the appropriate categories.*

unforgettable	charming	henpecked	tremendous	~~dignity~~
encouraging	frustrating	tension	confused	limited
opportunity	satisfying	comforting	imperfection	believable
ambition	comforted	humorous	well dressed	

-ity	-ion	-ing	-ed	-ous	-able
dignity					

Now, label each suffix with the part of speech it can change a word into: noun, verb, or adjective. Use your dictionary to help you.

-ity	-ion	-ing	-ed	-ous	-able
noun					

2 *Rewrite the sentences below using the new word form in parentheses. Keep the meaning of the original sentence.*

1. When Lucille Ball and Desi Arnaz had the opportunity to create a TV show, they experienced confusion at first. (confused)

   When Lucille Ball and Desi Arnaz had the opportunity to create a TV show, they felt confused at first.

2. Lucille Ball had an encouraging dream. (encouragement)

   _____

3. It takes ambition to become a successful doctor like Cliff Huxtable. (ambitious)

   _____

4. People in the *I Love Lucy* audience felt tense when Lucy got in trouble. (tension)

_____

5. Ricky Ricardo always kept his dignity even though his wife played tricks on him. (dignified)

_____

6. *I Love Lucy* and *The Cosby Show* were both humorous TV shows. (humor)

_____

7. One of the things that made *I Love Lucy* and *The Cosby Show* successful was that people identified with Cliff and Lucy's imperfections. (imperfect)

_____

8. Ricky had a satisfying career as a bandleader. (satisfied)

_____

9. Although Lucy knew that Ricky loved her, she also knew how limited his patience was. (limit)

_____

10. We identify with Cliff's imperfections and are comforted to see that someone loves him anyway. (comforting)

_____

3 *Write a summary of what you have learned about the differences in the humor of the 1950s and of the 1980s using at least five of the words below. You may change the form of the words.*

tension	opportunity	imperfection	bicker
encouraging	dignity	deal with	humorous
limitation	scene	ambitious	satisfied

4 Focus on Writing

1 *Read the following sentences taken from "The Story of* I Love Lucy.*" Label the subjects and verbs in each sentence.*

Desi clearly described and carefully summarized what his ideas for the show were.

Ricky and Lucy would be very much in love with each other and would never flirt with other characters.

Writers use **parallel structure** when they put two or three words or phrases of the same part of speech together in a series. The use of parallel structure allows writers to express several ideas in one sentence and to express these ideas clearly.

- I think this tension between **feeling loved** and **feeling afraid** made the show **more exciting** and **funnier** to watch.
- Instead, Dr. Huxtable **relaxes** at home in a sweater and **does** simple, fatherly things.

Two ideas can be expressed in one sentence:

- When he **raises** his eyebrows, we know that everything is going to be all right.
- When he **smiles,** we know that everything is going to be all right.
- When he **raises** his eyebrows and **smiles,** we know that everything is going to be all right.

A third idea can be added:

- When he **chuckles,** we know that everything is going to be all right.
- When he **raises** his eyebrows, **smiles,** and **chuckles,** we know that everything is going to be all right.

Notice that *raises, smiles,* and *chuckles* are all present tense verbs.

Now look at the following two examples:

- Desi **clearly described** and **carefully summarized** what his ideas for the show were. (The phrases are parallel because both phrases contain an adverb and a verb.)
- We trusted their **good writing skills** and **wonderful sense of humor.** (The phrases are parallel because both phrases contain an adjective and a noun.)

2 *Use parallel structure to combine the sentences below.*

1. **a.** *I Love Lucy* was exciting to watch.

   b. *I Love Lucy* was surprising to watch.

   _____

2. **a.** The show's writers worked carefully together.

   b. The show's writers worked closely together.

   _____

3. **a.** Theo's sisters think that he is irresponsible with money.

   b. Theo's parents think that he is irresponsible with money.

   _____

4. **a.** We identify with Cliff's imperfections.

   b. We are comforted to see that someone loves him anyway.

   _____

5. **a.** In a perfect world, both husband and wife have satisfying, high-paid careers.

   b. They still have time and energy to love their kids.

   c. They are able to laugh.

   _____

6. **a.** If we chuckle our way through our problems, things are going to be OK.

   b. If we love the people around us, things are going to be OK.

   _____

7. **a.** I just noticed that a certain person said, "Can I borrow that jacket?"

   b. Then, I just noticed that a certain person proceeded to wear that jacket every single day.

   _____

8. **a.** All episodes are based on real day-to-day problems.

   b. All episodes handle the problems with humor.

   _____

3 Now describe a humorous TV show or movie that you like. Complete the paragraph below. Use parallel structure.

Humorous Entertainment

I enjoy watching _____.
(name of the TV show or movie)

It is _____, _____, and _____.
ADJ   ADJ   ADJ

The actors are talented because they can perform _____ and
ADV

_____. The audience likes to watch them _____
ADV   V

and _____. I especially like it because of its _____
V   ADJ

_____ and _____ _____.
N   ADJ   N

B   GRAMMAR: Noun Clauses with *Wh-* words

1 Read the following paragraph taken from "The Story of I Love Lucy." Notice the two underlined phrases. Can you find any similarities in the structure of the underlined phrases?

Desi clearly described and carefully summarized <u>what his ideas for the show were</u>. He told CBS that the show's humor would never be mean or unkind. Ricky and Lucy would be very much in love with each other and would never flirt with other characters. Most of all, Ricky would always keep his dignity as a man. He told the writers not to let Lucy surprise him. "If Lucy's going to play a trick on me, make it clear to the audience that Ricky knows <u>what's going on</u>."

Now look at the sentences below taken from Readings One and Two. Label the boldfaced parts of the sentences as **Wh-** for the Wh- word, **S** for the subject, and **V** for the verb.

Example

- When people think of *I Love Lucy*, the slapstick comedy is usually **what they remember**.

- But this was also the first chance that Desi and I had to work together, and this was exactly **what we wanted to do**.

- . . . we know **what they are thinking**: You're a pain in the neck, but I still love you.

- **What America needs to see right now** is a happy family.

Noun Clauses with *Wh-* Words

1. A noun clause is a subject-verb combination. It can begin with a *wh-* word (*who, what, when, where, why, how*) followed by a subject and verb.

Ricky knew **when Lucy was playing a trick on him.**

2. At the beginning of a sentence, a noun clause is the subject. After the main verb, a noun clause is the object.

What America needs to see is a happy family.
A happy family is **what America needs to see.**

3. The verb tense in the noun clause usually follows the verb tense of the main clause.

Cliff **knew** why Theo **asked** for an advance on his allowance. (Past)

…**I know** what kind of man Mr. Cosby **is**—he is too smart to care. (Present)

Look at the following questions and answers. How does the word order change? How does the verb change?

What is he like?

I don't know **what he is like.**

What are they thinking?

I don't know **what they are thinking.**
We know **what they are thinking.**

What does America need to see right now?

What America needs to see right now is a happy family.

Notice that in the question the verb *be* or the auxiliary verb comes before the subject, but in a noun clause the subject comes before the verb.

2 *Betty and Mary are sisters watching* I Love Lucy *together. Read their conversation. Then complete the sentences that follow with a noun clause. Pay attention to verb tense.*

Betty: Who's that lady? Is that Lucy?

Mary: Yeah. Watch her. She's really funny.

Betty: And the other one—is that her neighbor? What's her name?

Mary: That's Ethel. She's Lucy's best friend.

Betty: Lucy seems worried. Is she always that way?

Mary: Not always. I think she's worried because her husband Ricky's coming home from work soon. She's probably in trouble again.

Betty: Where does he work? In his office nearby?

Mary: No. He's a bandleader. He works in a nightclub.

Betty: Wow. How exciting!

Mary: I know. It is exciting. And it's funny to watch Lucy try to work in the nightclub, too. She does that because she wants to be in show business.

Sentence Completion

1. Betty wants to know who _____ .

2. Betty wants to know what _____ .

3. Lucy knows when Ricky usually _____ , and this makes her nervous.

4. Betty asks where _____ .

5. The *I Love Lucy* show is what Mary and Betty _____ .

6. Wanting to be in show business is why _____ .

3 *Use the sentence starters below to express questions you have about the* I Love Lucy *show or* The Cosby Show.

1. I want to know when _____ .

2. I want to know where _____ .

3. I wonder who _____ .

4. I want to know why _____ .

5. I don't know how _____ .

Use the prompts below to express your ideas about what you have read. Write your own sentence in item 8. Include a noun clause.

6. _____ is why the critics said *The Cosby Show* would be a hit.

7. What the TV critic said was interesting to me because _____
_____ .

8. _____ .

C | WRITING TOPICS

Write two or three paragraphs on one of the following topics. Use some of the vocabulary, grammar, and style that you learned in this unit.

1. Do you prefer humorous or serious TV shows? Explain.

2. Does it help people to watch happy families on TV, or does it give them a false idea about life? Explain.

3. Can people of all countries share the same humor? Explain.

4. How has humor changed from the 1950s to the 1980s to the present?

D | RESEARCH TOPIC

Find out about other comedy stars. Below are some choices:

Cantinflas (Mexico)	Carol Burnett (United States)
Jim Carrey (United States)	Stephen Chow (Hong Kong)
Will Smith (United States)	Another comedian (from any country)
Rajindernath (India)	

Step 1: Choose one of the comedians above that you want to know more about.

Step 2: Find information about the comedian, and write a biography (life story) of this person. Try to answer these questions:

- What kind of childhood did this person have?

- Did this person dream of being in show business?

- How and when did this person become a star?

- What kind of humor is this person famous for: jokes, slapstick, or both?

- Do you think this person has had or had a happy life? Why or why not?

Step 3: Share your biography with the class.

For step-by-step practice in the writing process, see *Writing Activity Book, Intermediate,*
Unit 7.

Assignment	Descriptive Essay
Prewriting	Answering Questions
Organizing	Outlining
Revising	Writing Introductions and Conclusions
	Using Noun Clauses with *wh-* words
Editing	Using Parallel Structure

For Unit 7 Internet activities, visit the NorthStar Companion Website at
http://www.longman.com/northstar.

Always in Fashion

Cosmetic Surgery
The Beautiful People's Secret

1 Focus on the Topic

A PREDICTING

Look at the magazine ad, and discuss these questions with the class.

1. What is cosmetic surgery? Do you think this type of surgery is painful?

2. Do you know anyone who has had this kind of surgery?

3. How much do you think it costs?

B   SHARING INFORMATION

Complete this survey. Circle the letter that best matches your opinion. Compare your answers in small groups. On which statements did you have a similar opinion? On which statements did you have a different opinion?

SURVEY
A = Strongly Agree   B = Agree   C = Disagree   D = Strongly Disagree

1. Fashion is a very important part of today's society.		A B C D
2. People pay too much attention to new clothing styles.		A B C D
3. People spend too much time and money on the way they look.		A B C D
4. People feel happier when they look good.		A B C D
5. Most people wish they could change the way they look.		A B C D
6. Most people choose their friends because of the way they look.		A B C D

C   PREPARING TO READ

BACKGROUND

Look at the information on the timeline. Then discuss the following questions as a class.

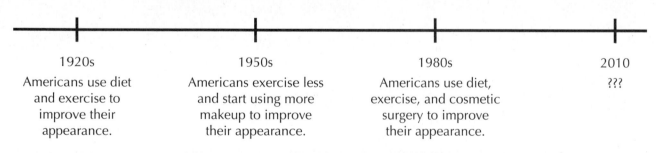

1920s	1950s	1980s	2010
Americans use diet and exercise to improve their appearance.	Americans exercise less and start using more makeup to improve their appearance.	Americans use diet, exercise, and cosmetic surgery to improve their appearance.	???

1. How did the American idea of beauty change in the 1950s? How did it change in the 1980s? How will it change by 2010?

2. Some people use cosmetic surgery to change the way their bodies look. Do you think this is better than diet and exercise? Why or why not?

3. What kind of diet helps to improve a person's appearance? What types of exercise help people look better?

VOCABULARY FOR COMPREHENSION

Study the definitions. Then read the passage, and complete the sentences with one of the vocabulary words. Use each word only once.

> **admire:** to have a good opinion of someone or something
> **appearance:** the way someone or something looks
> **attractive:** good-looking
> **desire:** a hope or wish
> **height:** how tall a person is
> **ideal:** perfect; the idea of what is perfect
> **modern:** part of today's world
> **permanent:** unchanging; staying the same
> **popular:** liked by many people
> **slim:** thin; not overweight
> **traditional:** relating to the past
> **weight:** how heavy a person is

Fashion, or clothing style, is always changing. Fashion is never (1) _____. Long skirts, short skirts, pants for women, makeup and earrings for men—these are some of the fashions that come in and out of style. A style that is (2) _____ one year is out of style the next.

In many countries today, people wear (3) _____ fashions most of the time. They sometimes wear their (4) _____ clothing on special days such as holidays. For example, in Japan, people often wear kimonos, or long silk dresses, on New Year's Day. Yet fashion is more than clothing. If you look at fashion magazines, you see many tall, (5) _____ models. These models show that (6) _____ and (7) _____ are an important part of fashion. Many people (8) _____ fashion models and wish that they could look more like them. As long as people have the (9) _____ to be beautiful, there will be fashion. There will always be people who follow the latest styles because they want to look their best and be more (10) _____. These people think that their (11) _____ is very important. They will spend much of their time and money trying to look like the (12) _____ man or woman.

2 Focus on Reading

A   READING ONE: *The Search for Beauty*

The passage below comes from a chapter in a book about cosmetic surgery. Read the first paragraph, and then use the space below to write what you already know about fashions in the past. How have clothing styles changed? How have people's ideas about diet and exercise changed? How has the idea of beauty changed?

_____

_____

_____

_____

_____

_____

_____

_____

Share what you have written with the class. Then continue reading "The Search for Beauty."

THE SEARCH FOR
BEAUTY

1   Cosmetic surgery, also known as "plastic" surgery, is the science of changing the way a person looks by reshaping a part of the body. Cosmetic surgery also includes replacing the skin of people who have been burned and replacing the hair that some people lose as they grow older. The science of beauty has changed with time, but the desire for beauty remains the same. This chapter will discuss how fashions have changed and how these changes have led to the new modern age of cosmetic surgery.

2   People have always had the desire to look more beautiful and fashionable. Whatever their age, size, or shape, people have followed fashion in order to look more attractive. In the 1800s, for example, American women in New York used to admire the fashions of Paris. In fact, since

French fashions were so popular, American dressmakers used to change their names to French ones!

3   In the 1700s, height and weight became an important part of beauty. During the time of the French Revolution, many women used to wear corsets, belts that made their waists appear much slimmer. Men used to admire women with small waists. Today, we still think of the ideal person as tall and slim. But nowadays, men or women who want to change their body shapes don't need to wear uncomfortable clothing. Instead, they can choose cosmetic surgery to reshape their bodies or to remove body fat.

4   In England in the 1500s, makeup became an important part of beauty. Thus, some women used to paint their faces white. They thought this made them more attractive. Later, in North America, some women used to eat arsenic, a dangerous poison, to make their faces whiter. By the 1860s, American women started using makeup to make themselves more attractive. These days, women who want to look their best at all times have started using permanent makeup. Some men, especially those in show business, also use permanent makeup. The application of permanent makeup is a type of cosmetic surgery. It is much safer than using paint and arsenic, and it helps busy people save time.

5   In the 1890s, Americans discovered that bicycle riding could actually improve their appearance! They exercised in order to look and feel better. The popularity of bicycle riding even led to a change in fashion. American women didn't use to wear pants back then. However, when bicycle riding became popular, they began to wear shorter skirts instead of the traditional long, full ones they used to wear. By the 1920s, the beauty ideal was closely related to health, and people believed that diet and exercise were the best ways to become naturally beautiful.

6   Although diet and exercise are still popular ways of improving one's appearance, there are some parts of the body that cannot change without the help of a cosmetic surgeon. In the past, American women used to spend weeks repeating words that started with the letter "p" because they wanted to change the shape of their mouths. Today, a cosmetic surgeon can reshape the nose or lips in a few hours. Rhinoplasty, the reshaping of the nose, can greatly improve a person's appearance. People who cannot lose weight in certain areas of their bodies through diet and exercise can use liposuction, the surgical removal of body fat, to make their bodies slimmer.

7   Surprisingly, cosmetic surgery has been used for centuries in China and India. In India in the sixth century, noses were re-created with plastic surgery after they had been cut off as a punishment. Today, cosmetic surgery is used in many countries to improve the appearance of people who have been hurt in fires or in car accidents. Cosmetic surgery is also used to improve the appearance of children who are born with physical problems.

8 Is it possible that in the future everyone will look more beautiful? The answer could be yes. Cosmetic surgeons are working hard to find safer and faster ways to help people who want to change the way they look. With the help of computers, people can see their new faces before the surgery is even done. With lasers,[1] cosmetic surgery can be done faster than ever before. And people from all over the world fly into countries like Costa Rica, the Dominican Republic, and Brazil, where cosmetic surgery is a growing business. However, like any form of surgery, cosmetic surgery can be dangerous and painful. It is also somewhat expensive for the average person. Consequently, cosmetic surgery is not as popular today as it could be in the future. As surgeons perfect their techniques so that they become safer, faster, and less expensive, people around the world will continue their search for beauty.

[1] *lasers:* machines that produce very strong light

READING FOR MAIN IDEAS

Look at "The Search for Beauty" again to find sentences with similar meanings to the sentences below. Next to each sentence, write the paragraph number where you found a similar sentence. Share your answers with the class.

_____ **a.** People admired the fashions of foreign countries.

_____ **b.** Cosmetic surgery is becoming safer and faster.

_____ **c.** Women tried to change the shape of their bodies.

_____ **d.** Cosmetic surgery is not a modern science.

_____ **e.** People believed that health was an important part of beauty.

_____ **f.** Becoming beautiful may be easier in the future.

READING FOR DETAILS

*Write **T** (true) or **F** (false) for each statement according to the reading. Then change the false statements to true ones.*

_____ **1.** Paris was the example of fashion in the 1800s.

_____ **2.** Women in France wanted to have larger waists.

_____ **3.** Corsets were not comfortable.

_____ **4.** Some women used paint to change the color of their faces.

_____ **5.** Some men today wear permanent makeup.

_____ **6.** Liposuction is often used to add body fat.

_____ **7.** Cosmetic surgery is a modern science.

_____ **8.** Children are not too young for cosmetic surgery.

_____ **9.** Some women tried to reshape their eyes by doing exercises.

_____ **10.** Some people may die during cosmetic surgery.

_____ **11.** Cosmetic surgery is inexpensive.

REACTING TO THE READING

1 *Complete the sentences by using information from Reading One. Make a good guess based on your understanding of the information. Share your sentences with the class.*

1700s: During the French Revolution, women <u>*wore corsets to look thinner*</u>

_____.

1800s: American women admired French fashions because _____

_____.

1890s: People who rode bicycles _____

_____.

1990s: Men who lose their hair _____

_____.

2025: Cosmetic surgery will _____

_____.

2 *Look at Reading One again. Pick the time period of fashion that you think represents the most interesting attitudes toward fashion. What is interesting about this period to you? Why? What surprised you? Write for five minutes. Then discuss your ideas with a classmate.*

B   READING TWO: *My Wife Wants to Look Younger*

1 *Read the following journal pages written by a man whose wife decided to have a face-lift (a form of cosmetic surgery that makes people look younger).*

Monday, April 4

Susan came home today with some surprising news. She says she feels too young on the inside to look like a tired old grandma. Therefore, she wants to get a face-lift! (I thought coloring her hair made enough of a difference, but no, she wants a whole new face.) I told her that we have to meet with the doctor first. I don't want her to go into the surgery without knowing the dangers.

Tuesday, April 12

Today we sat down and talked it over with a surgeon. It's simple. The doctor cuts open the skin around the face, lifts the skin up and pulls it back, and cuts off the extra skin. And, as a result, there you are, ten years younger. I watched Susan carefully while the doctor was explaining all this, and it didn't seem to discourage her. I asked about the pain, and the doctor said not to expect any during surgery because of the painkiller that he'll use. It seems like doctors have all kinds of pain-killing medicine these days. After the surgery, the doctor said there might be four or five days of "discomfort." That's what he called it. I notice that he doesn't use the word "pain."

Thursday, April 14

Susan and I stayed up late last night making our decision. We're going to do it. I told her that it doesn't matter to me at all. I love her no matter what. (Also, I don't want her to expect some fantastic change in our marriage just because she looks younger.) The doctor mentioned that, too. He said it's important not to expect too much from the surgery. Susan will look younger—that's all. It's not going to bring her instant happiness. Susan understands this. She just wants to look as young as she feels. And I wouldn't mind having a wife who looks a little younger. Who would? I just hope she won't find a younger man. Maybe I should ask the doctor if he can do anything about my bald head.

Wednesday, April 20

Susan had a medical interview today. The doctor wanted to know about her lifestyle. Susan was so glad she finally quit smoking as she could tell the doc that she's "smoke-free" and feeling good. Plus, she's more or less at her ideal weight. Due to the fact that her face is going to look pretty bad after surgery, the doctor wanted to know how she felt about her face being black and blue for a few weeks. She told him, "Look, I've had five kids. Do you think a funny-looking face is going to scare me?" The doctor laughed and said she's in good shape physically and mentally, and I agree. Two weeks from today—that's how long we have to wait. I'm starting to wonder what she's going to look like.

Thursday, May 5

Today's the big day. Susan's in surgery right now. She'll be in surgery for about six hours—three hours on each side of her face. It was interesting to watch the doctor take a pen and mark up her face, drawing lines for the knife to follow. Knife! Poor Susan. I hope she'll be OK.

Thursday, May 19

What a crazy time it's been! We had to put bags of frozen strawberries over her eyes, and that really helped her get better. And I can't believe her face—so young and smooth. She looks fifteen years younger, and she feels great. I can see this in the way she walks and in how she spends a little more time with her makeup in the morning. The doctor says she'll look this way for about ten more years. Too bad it's not permanent. But if Susan wants to do this again, why not? I think it's worth it.

2 *Discuss these questions with the class.*

1. What kind of person do you think Susan is?

2. Do you think Susan and her husband have a good relationship? Why or why not?

3. What are some of the risks involved in cosmetic surgery? Would any of these risks stop you from having surgery?

4. Why do you think the doctor uses the word *discomfort* instead of *pain*? How will Susan avoid pain during the surgery?

3 *In the space below, write three or four sentences that might appear in Susan's husband's journal before or after her surgery. Share your writing with a partner.*

_____
_____
_____
_____
_____
_____

C LINKING READINGS ONE AND TWO

Look at Reading One again. Then explain how cosmetic surgery can help the people in Susan's life (see below). In addition to cosmetic surgery, what are some other ways they can improve their appearance? Work with a partner to write your answers. Then share them with the class.

1. her bald husband

_____
_____

2. her older sister

_____
_____

3. her friend who cannot lose weight

_____
_____

4. her brother who wants to have a more handsome face

_____
_____

5. her neighbor who was burned in a fire

_____
_____

3 Focus on Vocabulary

1 *Look at the following nouns taken from Readings One and Two. Which of these nouns can be used with the adjectives below? Some nouns can be used more than once.*

music	appearance	surgery	hair	color	personality	style
weight	relationship	height	body	man	makeup	

1. ideal: *man, body, relationship, personality*

2. modern/traditional: _____

3. popular: _____

4. attractive: _____

5. slim: _____

6. permanent: _____

7. fashionable: _____

8. painful: _____

2 *Use the underlined words to express your own ideas about a different topic. The words in parentheses give you the new topic.*

1. For me, the <u>ideal</u> vacation would be going to Hawaii and swimming in the ocean. (body)

   For me, the ideal body is muscular and thin, but not too thin.

2. The person I <u>admire</u> most is my father because he is very intelligent. (writer)

   _____

3. If you want to see <u>popular</u> fashion styles, try looking in a fashion magazine. (sports)

   _____

4. In some countries, white is a <u>traditional</u> color for a bride. (ceremonies)

   _____

5. I think people who smile a lot are very <u>attractive</u>. (long hair)

   _____

6. I love <u>modern</u> art, but some people can't stand it. (buildings)

_____

7. One of my <u>desires</u> is to visit Australia. (learn)

_____

8. His <u>appearance</u> made me think he was a rebel. (rich)

_____

9. It is <u>physically</u> impossible for humans to walk to the moon. (fly)

_____

10. Some people, when they first wake up, are not <u>mentally</u> alert. (other people)

_____

3 *Suppose that you have a close friend who wants to meet someone and get married. However, your friend feels unattractive in some way. He or she is considering cosmetic surgery in order to "catch" a husband or wife. If that friend asked for your opinion, what would you say? Write a letter to him or her using at least five of the words below.*

ideal	attractive	admire	appearance	desire
physically	mentally	beautiful	popular	permanent

4 Focus on Writing

A   STYLE: Cause and Effect

1 *Look at the sentences taken from Readings One and Two. What do the underlined words mean?*

> In fact, <u>since</u> French fashions were so popular, American dressmakers used to change their names to French ones!

> In the past, American women used to spend weeks repeating words that started with the letter "p" <u>because</u> they wanted to change the shape of their mouths.

> . . . cosmetic surgery can be dangerous and painful. It is also somewhat expensive for the average person. <u>Consequently</u>, cosmetic surgery is not as popular today as it could be in the future.

> She says she feels too young on the inside to look like a tired old grandma. <u>Therefore</u>, she wants to get a face-lift!

Writers use **transitions** to help readers move from one idea to the next. These words or phrases prepare the reader for what type of information will come next. Different transitions are used to show cause and effect. Notice that these transitions are used with a complete sentence containing a subject and verb.

Transitions Used to Show Cause

because   *since*   *as*

- In fact, **since** French fashions were so popular, American dressmakers used to change their names to French ones!

- In the past, American women used to spend weeks repeating words that started with the letter "p" **because** they wanted to change the shape of their mouths.

- Susan was so glad she finally quit smoking **as** she could tell the doc that she's "smoke-free" and feeling good.

Transitions Used to Show Effect

therefore   *consequently*   *thus*   *as a result*

- In England in the 1500s, makeup became an important part of beauty. **Thus,** some women used to paint their faces white.

- …cosmetic surgery can be dangerous and painful. It is also somewhat expensive for the average person. **Consequently,** cosmetic surgery is not as popular today as it could be in the future.

- She says she feels too young on the inside to look like a tired old grandma. **Therefore,** she wants to get a face-lift!

- The doctor cuts open the skin around the face, lifts the skin up and pulls it back, and cuts off the extra skin. And, **as a result,** there you are, ten years younger.

2 *Read the paragraph below about an actor who updates* his wardrobe.** Complete the sentences with the best choice of transition. You may need to add commas to some sentences.*

Saving the Clothes in Your Closet

Evan Buckley had a closet full of clothes but little to wear. (**1.** Since / As a result) _____, he got fashion stylist David Romero to help him

---

* **update:** to make something that is out of style look new
** **wardrobe:** all of a person's clothes

and now has a more stylish and youthful wardrobe. "I'm a pack rat[1] with a huge closet, but I always walk into it and say 'I have nothing to wear.'" He felt that part of his problem was that (**2.** consequently / since) _____ he is a TV newscaster and has to dress like a newscaster every day, he had forgotten his own personal style. (**3.** As / Thus) _____ Buckley felt it was time to update his wardrobe. "The thirties are the best time of your life (**4.** because / thus) _____ you know who you are and you're still physically young. I want that to show in the clothes I wear." (**5.** As / Consequently) _____, he called Romero to help him out. Romero's advice was not to buy a whole new wardrobe. He thought they could keep some items if they changed them a little bit. They would (**6.** because / therefore) _____ need a tailor[2] for some items. Then they would shop for some new things to go with what Buckley already had. A shirt that was too old-fashioned was given a new collar. A pair of pinstriped pants was updated with a new shirt. Evan was so glad he finally asked someone to help him (**7.** as / therefore) _____ he now has a whole new wardrobe. "David has a good sense of style," says Buckley. Now, (**8.** as a result / since) _____, so does Evan Buckley.

3 *Look at "My Wife Wants to Look Younger" again. Write five sentences using transitions of cause and effect about the information you learned.*

Example: <u>Susan wants to have a face-lift because she feels too young to</u>
<u>look like an old grandmother.</u>

1. _____

2. _____

3. _____

4. _____

5. _____

---

[1] *pack rat:* a person who never throws anything away
[2] *tailor:* a person who makes or adjusts clothes

B   GRAMMAR: Describing the Past with *Used to*

1 *Read the following sentences from Reading One. What is the meaning of* used to?

> In fact, since French fashions were so popular, American dressmakers <u>used to</u> change their names to French ones!

> Thus, some women <u>used to</u> paint their faces white.

> In the past, American women <u>used to</u> spend weeks repeating words that started with the letter "p" because they wanted to change the shape of their mouths.

Describing the Past with *Used to*

1. *Used to* can describe habits or customs in the past that are not followed anymore. Habits are actions that are repeated regularly, such as putting on makeup in the morning or getting a haircut once a month.	Later, in North America, some women **used to** eat arsenic, a dangerous poison, to make their faces whiter. However, when bicycle riding became popular, they began to wear shorter skirts instead of the traditional long, full ones they **used to** wear. Many women **used to** wear corsets, belts that made their waists appear slimmer.
2. *Used to* can also describe people's attitudes in the past.	In the 1800s, for example, American women in New York **used to** admire the fashions of Paris. Men **used to** admire women with small waists.
3. The negative is formed this way: ***didn't use to.***	American women **didn't use to** wear pants back then.

2 *Look at the picture. Complete the following sentences with the correct form of* **used to** *or* **didn't use to.**

1. In the 1920s, Americans _____ believe that natural beauty was the best.

2. They _____ exercise in order to improve their appearance.

3. Women at that time _____ have very short, simple hairstyles.

4. They _____ spend a lot of time styling their hair or putting on makeup.

3 *Think about a fashion that you used to wear in the past. It can be clothing, shoes, or a hairstyle. Describe it in detail below.*

In the past, I used to _____

_____

_____

_____

_____

_____

_____

_____

_____

_____

I didn't use to _____ as I do today.

4 *Interview a classmate about fashions that she or he wore in the past or about fashions that people wore a long time ago in a certain part of the world. Then write a paragraph based on information from the interview. Use the simple past tense as well as the* used to *form.*

Example

When Hiro was a child, he used to wear a school uniform. His shorts were blue, and his shirt was white. On rainy days he used to wear a blue sweater and carry a black umbrella. In the mornings, his mother used to comb his hair. His hair was very thick and straight. His mother often combed it hard to get out the tangles. Hiro didn't use to like this.

_____

_____

_____

_____

_____

_____

_____

_____

C WRITING TOPICS

Choose one of the following topics. Write two or three paragraphs, using some of the vocabulary, grammar, and style that you learned in this unit.

1. Describe something that has changed in your life as a result of moving to a new place, or something that has changed with the passing of time.

2. Most people believe that the teenage years are a time when young people are very concerned about looking good. How did you feel about your appearance when you were a teenager? What advice would you give to teenagers who feel that they are unattractive?

3. How do you feel about growing older? What have you learned from your life? In what ways has growing older changed you?

4. They say that trends in fashions repeat themselves, that they are cyclical. Find a trend that occurred in the past and has been repeated recently. How is that repeated trend the same as in the past? How is it different from the past?

D RESEARCH TOPIC

Explore the world of clothing fashion by visiting a local department store.

Step 1: Work in small groups. Choose one type of fashion that your group would like to examine (men's wear, women's wear, sportswear, formal wear, or something else). Visit that department in the store, and use the following form to record what you discover there.

Department:

Clothing Items:

Colors:

Styles:

(continued)

Price range (lowest to highest):

Quality:

Other Comments:

Step 2: Write a report of your findings, using some vocabulary words that you learned in this unit.

Step 3: Finally, exchange your report with members of another group. Discuss your reports together after you have read them.

For step-by-step practice in the writing process, see *Writing Activity Book, Intermediate,* Unit 8.

Assignment	Expository Essay
Prewriting	Clustering
Organizing	Definition and Opinion Paragraphs
Revising	Refining Statements of Fact
	Using *Used to*
Editing	Correcting Sentence Fragments

For Unit 8 Internet activities, visit the NorthStar Companion Website at http://www.longman.com/northstar.

UNIT **9**

Crime and Punishment

1 Focus on the Topic

A PREDICTING

First look at the photograph, and discuss these questions: What are the people doing? Where are they? What do their signs mean?

Now look at the list of words. Underline the words that are the most closely related to the photograph.

crime	opinion	justice	disagreement
agreement	murder	punishment	execution
government	protest	doctor	education

155

B   SHARING INFORMATION

Discuss the following questions in small groups.

1. Capital punishment means taking the life of someone who has committed a crime. How many forms of capital punishment do you know about?

2. In the United States, capital punishment is allowed in some states. Do you know of any other societies in which capital punishment is allowed?

3. Why do some people believe that capital punishment is fair? Why do others think that it is unfair?

C   PREPARING TO READ

BACKGROUND

Work in small groups. Discuss punishment in two different cultures. Complete the forms below. Check (✓) the answers.

Culture 1: _____

Punishment for murder:	○ Prison	○ Execution	○ Other: _____
Punishment for robbery:	○ Prison	○ Execution	○ Other: _____
Who pays for the punishment?	○ Taxpayers	○ Other: _____	
What do people do in prison?	○ Exercise	○ Read/Write	○ Do hard physical labor
	○ Receive physical punishment		○ Study/Take classes
	○ Other: _____		

Culture 2: _____

Punishment for murder:	○ Prison	○ Execution	○ Other: _____
Punishment for robbery:	○ Prison	○ Execution	○ Other: _____
Who pays for the punishment?	○ Taxpayers	○ Other: _____	
What do people do in prison?	○ Exercise	○ Read/Write	○ Do hard physical labor
	○ Receive physical punishment		○ Study/Take classes
	○ Other: _____		

VOCABULARY FOR COMPREHENSION

Read the sentences and the definitions below. Choose the best definition for the underlined words.

_____ 1. People who <u>murder</u> are very dangerous.

_____ 2. It is <u>cruel</u> to not give prisoners food or to keep them alone in the dark for many days.

_____ 3. The laws enforced by the courts require <u>justice</u> for every person.

_____ 4. Everyone wants other people to <u>respect</u> their freedom.

_____ 5. Everyone has the <u>right</u> to be treated fairly, and the laws must protect those rights.

_____ 6. In many countries, <u>citizenship</u> is given automatically to all children who are born there.

_____ 7. <u>Society</u> must find ways to stop crime.

_____ 8. He asked for <u>forgiveness</u> from the people he had hurt.

_____ 9. There are many laws that protect <u>innocent</u> children from danger.

_____ 10. Some people who are not <u>guilty</u> have gone to prison by mistake.

_____ 11. I heard about his murder on TV. It is terrible to think that he died such a <u>violent</u> death.

_____ 12. In some cultures, people seek <u>revenge</u> by hurting the person who has hurt them.

a. be careful not to do anything against someone's life or wishes

b. the rights and freedoms that belong to the members of a nation

c. having done something wrong

d. letting go of one's anger after someone has hurt you

e. the bad thing you do to someone because they did something bad to you

f. kill a human being on purpose

g. not having done something wrong

h. likely to hurt or kill someone

i. deliberately making someone suffer or feel unhappy

j. a large group of people who share the same laws and organizations

k. treatment of people which is fair and right

l. something that you are allowed to do or have according to the law

2 Focus on Reading

A newspaper editorial gives the writer's opinion about a topic. As with any news article, an editorial begins with a headline or title. Look at the following editorial headlines. On a separate piece of paper, write any ideas that you expect to find in each editorial. Then read the editorials.

Headline 1—Life in Prison Is Still Life: Why Should a Killer Live?

Headline 2—Why Do We Kill People to Show That Killing People Is Wrong?

Life in Prison Is Still Life: Why Should a Killer Live?

1   Murder is totally unfair; the victims of murder are gone forever. Their hopes and plans have ended permanently, and the pleasures they enjoyed in life have been destroyed. They will never see their friends again and will never hear the voices of parents, brothers, and sisters who cry, "How could this have happened?" But the murderer is still alive. Without capital punishment, murderers are allowed to participate in and enjoy life.

2   Today there are murderers in prisons all over the world. Most of them would rather spend their lives in prison than die. This is not surprising since the desire to live is normal and natural. In prison there are many small pleasures that one can enjoy every day: the feeling of warm sunshine, the taste of a hot meal, the comfort of sleep. The lifestyle in prison is not always harsh and cruel; many prisoners have the opportunity to continue their educations, play sports, enjoy movies, and receive visits from their loved ones.

3   There is no reason why a killer, a destroyer of life, should live. Justice requires that each person respect the rights and freedoms of every other person, or be punished for not doing so. The people who commit murder give up their rights to citizenship and life itself. Why should the tax money of citizens—including the victim's family—keep the killer alive? The only fair punishment is execution. Execution puts the killer away from society forever, stops him from killing again, and sends a strong message to others who might kill: Killers will not be allowed to live.

4   Let sunshine fall on those who respect life—not on those who destroy it.

Why Do We Kill People to Show That Killing People Is Wrong?

1   There are times when murder is not committed because of cruelty. People may kill for other reasons such as anger, misunderstanding, and fear. Everyone has made mistakes because of such feelings. For society, it is a serious mistake to take the life of someone who has killed because it teaches everyone that forgiveness is unnecessary.

2   The government has the difficult job of deciding who is innocent and who is guilty, and this job can never be done perfectly. If capital punishment is allowed, there always exists the possibility that an innocent person will be executed by mistake. When that happens, an even worse crime has been committed—the killing of an innocent person by the government. Then there is the fact that the poor and minorities get the death penalty more often than whites do. Furthermore, the idea that capital punishment stops criminals from committing murder is doubtful; studies have been unable to show that the fear of capital punishment stops someone from committing murder more than other punishments. And let us not forget that murdering the murderer is a violent act in itself; it is revenge.

3   The U.S. government once followed the example of Germany, Britain, France, and other nations that no longer execute their citizens—however, since 1977, our society has been allowing capital punishment again, at a high cost. We cannot imagine the pain of family members who have been waiting for years for the government's decision to execute or not execute their loved ones. It also costs the taxpayer millions of dollars more to execute a criminal than to imprison that criminal for life. Prison is a better form of punishment because it protects society and punishes criminals by taking away their freedom.

4   People can change, even people who have made terrible mistakes. Life in prison gives people the chance to change. Caryl Chessman is an example of someone who became a better person in prison. He taught other prisoners how to read, and he wrote several books. Before his execution, he wrote that he had finally learned not to hate.

5   Chessman learned this important lesson in prison. But a dead man learns nothing, and an executed person will never change. When a government kills, it is murdering hope.

READING FOR MAIN IDEAS

The two editorials express different opinions about capital punishment.

Opinion A: Execution is a better form of punishment than life in prison.
Opinion B: Life in prison is a better form of punishment than execution.

*Look at the main ideas below. Which were used to support Opinion A? Opinion B? Match them correctly by writing **A** or **B**. Look at Reading One again to make sure that your answers are based on information from the reading.*

_____ 1. Execution may cause an innocent person to die.

_____ 2. Prisoners are able to enjoy life, and this is not fair.

_____ 3. Not all people who kill are cruel.

_____ 4. Capital punishment is revenge.

_____ 5. A prisoner is no longer free.

_____ 6. People naturally want to live.

_____ 7. Racial prejudice affects capital punishment.

_____ 8. Prison can sometimes improve a person.

_____ 9. Execution may teach other people not to commit crimes.

_____ 10. Execution is more expensive than life imprisonment.

READING FOR DETAILS

Match the main ideas from the previous exercise with the details below. Write the number of the main idea next to the detail.

__3__ a. Some murders are mistakes, caused by anger or fear.

_____ b. The government spends millions of tax dollars on execution decisions.

_____ c. Most people would rather go to prison than be executed.

_____ d. Caryl Chessman learned not to hate while in prison.

_____ e. The message of execution is that murderers will not be allowed to live.

_____ f. The government can make mistakes when it decides if a person is guilty or not.

_____ g. Prisoners have the basic pleasures of eating and sleeping.

_____ h. Executing the murderer is a violent act.

REACTING TO THE READING

1 *Look back at the ideas you listed in Section 2A on page 158. Which ideas did you predict correctly? Discuss your predictions with the class.*

2 *What kind of person wrote "Life in Prison Is Still Life: Why Should a Killer Live?" Look at the following list of qualities, and circle two or three you think best describe this person.*

- believes in forgiveness
- cares about prisoners
- believes in fairness
- cares about victims
- hopes to change people
- wants to protect society

3 *What kind of person wrote "Why Do We Kill People to Show That Killing People Is Wrong?" Look at the following list of qualities, and circle two or three you think best describe this person.*

- cares about prison workers
- believes freedom is important
- cares about prisoners' families
- wants other countries to follow the United States
- believes mistakes are unusual
- hopes that people will change

4 *Consider the two editorials you read about capital punishment. Discuss the pros and cons in small groups. List them on the chart below. Then form different small groups, and share your charts.*

CAPITAL PUNISHMENT	
Pro	Con

On a separate piece of paper, write a paragraph that gives your opinion on capital punishment.

B   READING TWO: Graphs

Look at the following four graphs. Titles, captions, and notes near a graph contain important information. Remember to study this information in order to interpret the graphs correctly. Then work with a classmate to answer the questions below each graph.

GRAPH 1

Death Penalty Facts

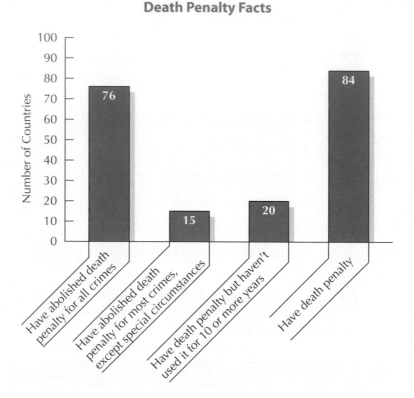

Source: List of Abolitionist and Retentionist Countries,
Amnesty International Index, 2002 (www.amnesty.org).

1. When were these facts published?

2. How many countries have *not* used the death penalty in recent times? Why do you think this is so?

3. Are most of these countries for or against the death penalty? Explain.

4. Can you use these facts to explain how the death penalty is used in a country you know well?

In March 2002, Zogby International surveyed voters in Albany County, New York with the following results, as shown in graphs 2 and 3.

GRAPH 2

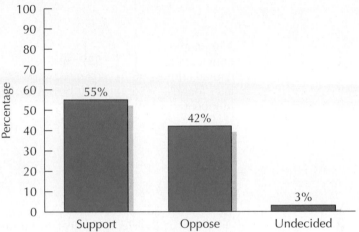

Do you support or oppose capital punishment for murderers?

Source: Zogby International, March 25, 2002.

GRAPH 3

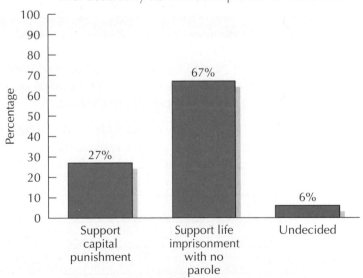

Do you support capital punishment, or life imprisonment with absolutely no chance of parole for murderers?

Source: Zogby International, March 25, 2002.

5. Why did the number of voters who support capital punishment drop from 55% in Graph 2 to 27% in Graph 3?

6. What conclusion can you make from these graphs?

GRAPH 4

Execution of the Innocent in the United States
1900–1992

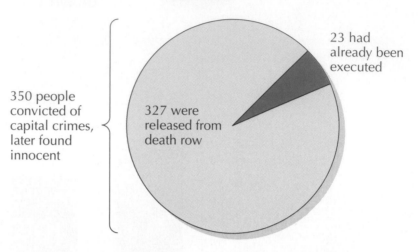

350 people convicted of capital crimes, later found innocent

327 were released from death row

23 had already been executed

Source: From *In Spite of Innocence* by Michael Radelet et al, 1994, as on Amnesty USA Website.

7. What does this information show about the capital punishment system in the United States?

8. Can anything be learned from this information? Explain.

C LINKING READINGS ONE AND TWO

Writers often need to support their opinions with facts and data. Use information from the graphs in Reading Two to support the opinions below from the editorials in Reading One. Add a sentence or two about the data.

1. There is no reason why a killer, a destroyer of life, should live. Justice requires that each person respect the rights and freedoms of every other person, or be punished for not doing so. (**Pro**)

_____

_____

_____

_____

2. If capital punishment is allowed, there always exists the possibility that an innocent person will be executed by mistake. When that happens, an even worse crime has been committed—the killing of an innocent person by the government. (**Con**)

_____

_____

_____

_____

3. The U.S. government once followed the example of Germany, Britain, France, and other nations that no longer execute their citizens—but since 1977, our society has been allowing capital punishment again. (**Pro or Con**)

_____

_____

_____

_____

3 Focus on Vocabulary

1 *Some nouns refer to ideas or feelings. They refer to things that cannot be seen or touched, such as* love *and* peace. *These nouns are called* **abstract nouns.** *Look at the following nouns, and mark the abstract nouns with* **A.** *Discuss your answers with the class.*

_____ 1. prison

_____ 2. friends

_____ 3. misunderstanding

_____ 4. anger

_____ 5. punishment

_____ 6. justice

_____ 7. family

_____ 8. food

_____ 9. citizenship

_____ 10. innocence

_____ 11. person

_____ 12. government

_____ 13. guilt

_____ 14. society

_____ 15. rights

2 *When writers use abstract nouns, they often use examples to help the reader understand more clearly what they mean. Match the examples on the left with the appropriate abstract noun on the right.*

_____ 1. cutting off the hand of a person who steals

_____ 2. a court has proof that someone is a murderer

_____ 3. deciding not to stay angry when someone has hurt you

_____ 4. considering a person innocent until proven guilty

_____ 5. choosing to do something that breaks the law

_____ 6. hurting an animal for no reason

_____ 7. carrying the passport of a particular country

_____ 8. relatives, friends, and neighbors

_____ 9. a court has proof that someone did not rob a bank

_____ 10. people moving from Mexico to California

a. forgiveness
b. cruelty
c. innocence
d. society
e. citizenship
f. guilt
g. immigration
h. punishment
i. fairness
j. crime

3 *In editorial writing, writers choose their words carefully. They want to present their opinions as strongly as possible so that the reader will agree with them. Look at the following pairs of sentences. Complete each sentence* **b** *by choosing one word to replace the underlined word in sentence* **a.** *How does the meaning change when you use a different word? Circle the strength of the new meaning, and discuss the variation in meanings with the class.*

1. a. A government is wrong when it <u>kills</u> its citizens.

b. A government is wrong when it _____ its citizens.
(punishes / executes)

New meaning: Weaker   Stronger   Neither

2. a. Why should we keep a <u>murderer</u> alive?

b. Why should we keep a _____ alive?
(criminal / guilty person)

New meaning: Weaker   Stronger   Neither

3. a. Life in prison is not always <u>bad</u>.

b. Life in prison is not always _____.
(fair / cruel)

New meaning: Weaker   Stronger   Neither

4. a. Prisoners hope to receive visits from the <u>people who care about them</u>.

b. Prisoners hope to receive visits from their _____.
(loved ones / relatives)

New meaning: Weaker   Stronger   Neither

5. a. Men and women who follow the laws of their country are usually good <u>people</u>.

    b. Men and women who follow the laws of their country are usually good

        _____ .
          (adults / citizens)

        New meaning: Weaker   Stronger   Neither

6. a. <u>Immigrants</u> are sometimes the victims of crime.

    b. _____ are sometimes the victims of crime.
        (Strangers / Foreigners)

        New meaning: Weaker   Stronger   Neither

7. a. Many people fear prison because they believe it will <u>hurt</u> their future.

    b. Many people fear prison because they believe it will _____
                                               (change / destroy)
    their future.

        New meaning: Weaker   Stronger   Neither

8. a. The murder was done out of <u>anger</u>.

    b. The murder was done out of _____ .
                            (passion / revenge)

        New meaning: Weaker   Stronger   Neither

4 *On a separate piece of paper, write one paragraph to answer the questions below. Use at least five of the words from the box in your response as well as any information you learned in this unit.*

murder	innocent	respect	punishment
forgive	justice	revenge	society
cruel	guilty	rights	violent

1. What do you predict will happen in the future with murderers?

2. Will punishment be more or less severe?

4 Focus on Writing

A STYLE: Sentence Variety

1 *Read the following passage. Look at the sentences carefully. How are they similar? How are they different?*

Murder is totally unfair because the victims of murder are gone forever. Their hopes and plans have ended permanently, and the pleasures they enjoyed in life have been destroyed. They will never see their friends again and will never hear the voices of their parents, brothers, and sisters. But the murderer is still alive. If we stop capital punishment, murderers will still be allowed to participate in life.

Writers often use different **sentence types** to make their writing more interesting. The three basic **sentence types** are **simple, compound,** and **complex.**

A **simple sentence** includes one subject and one verb.	The victims of murder are gone forever.
A **simple sentence** can also include a compound subject. This is a subject with two or more nouns.	Their hopes and plans have ended permanently.

A **compound sentence** consists of two clauses (subject-verb combinations). They are often joined with coordinating conjunctions (*and, but, or, so*). A comma is used before the coordinating conjunction.	I believe in capital punishment, but my sister doesn't. You are either in favor of the death penalty, or you are against it.

A **complex sentence** includes two clauses: independent and dependent. The independent clause (I.C.) is a complete sentence. It can stand alone. The dependent clause (D.C.) begins with a subordinating conjunction (*because, if, since, when, although*). The dependent clause is an incomplete sentence. It cannot stand alone.	Murder is unfair because the victims of murder are gone forever.

(continued)

A comma is used when the sentence begins with a dependent clause. It is not used when the sentence begins with an independent clause.

D.C.
If we stop capital punishment,
I.C.
murderers will still be allowed to participate in life.

2 *The following sentences describe the life of a death row prisoner named Wayne Paulson. Combine the two sentences into one compound or complex sentence. Use coordinating conjunctions (**and, but, or, so**) in compound sentences. Use subordinating conjunctions (**because, if, since, when, although**) in complex sentences. Be sure to use subject pronouns where appropriate.*

Example: a. Wayne Paulson reads books in prison.

b. Wayne Paulson sometimes exercises.

(or) *Wayne Paulson reads books in prison, or he sometimes exercises.*

1. **a.** Wayne Paulson was the kind of guy that was never noticed at school.

   b. Wayne Paulson wasn't the kind of guy that got into trouble.

   (and) _____

   _____

2. **a.** The police came to his house and arrested Wayne for murder.

   b. His life has never been the same.

   (since) _____

   _____

3. **a.** Wayne was found guilty at the end of his trial.

   b. He was given the death penalty.

   (because) _____

   _____

4. **a.** Wayne said that he is innocent.

   b. The jury didn't believe Wayne.

   (but) _____

   _____

5. **a.** Wayne still remembers his life before jail.

   b. Wayne's life in jail is very different now.

   (although) _____

   _____

6. **a.** Wayne's mother doesn't want him to feel lonely.

   b. She visits him almost every day.

   (so) _____

   _____

7. **a.** Some prisoners get new trials.

   b. Some prisoners like Wayne are able to leave prison.

   (if) _____

   _____

8. **a.** Wayne's lawyer visits him.

   b. Wayne asks about getting a new trial.

   (when) _____

   _____

3 *Read the following letter by an American college student taking a criminal justice class. On a separate piece of paper, rewrite the letter to use a variety of sentences: simple, compound, and complex. Make at least five changes, and change the sentence structure as much as you like.*

Dear Anne,

I'm taking a criminal justice class right now. We've been discussing capital punishment. I have really been shocked by some of the statistics we've learned! My classmates have really been shocked by some of the statistics we've learned! Did you know that in 1998 only four countries accounted for 80 percent of all executions worldwide? And did you know that the country which carried out the most executions of child criminals was the United States? It's true. The United States has executed ten since 1990. The United States plans to continue to execute child criminals.

I used to agree with capital punishment. I always thought that the fear of the death penalty stopped some criminals. That is false. Here is a quote I discovered. "Research has failed to provide proof that executions stop murders more than life imprisonment." But the fact that is the most difficult for me to accept is that between 1900 and 1992, 350 criminals who were sentenced to death were later found to be innocent. Twenty-three of those criminals were actually executed. That is a problem that always exists with capital punishment. Some of the prisoners are innocent. They get executed. There is no perfect way to find out if someone is guilty. I now disagree with capital punishment.

What do you think?

Your friend,

Katie

B   GRAMMAR: Contrast—Present Perfect and Present Perfect Progressive

1 *Read the following paragraphs taken from "Life in Prison Is Still Life: Why Should a Killer Live?" and "Why Do We Kill People to Show That Killing People Is Wrong?" There are two different verb tenses in bold. How are these tenses similar? How are they different?*

Murder is totally unfair; the victims of murder are gone forever. Their hopes and plans **have ended** permanently, and the pleasures they enjoyed in life have been destroyed. They will never see their friends again and will never hear the voices of parents, brothers, and sisters who cry, "How could this **have happened**?" But the murderer is still alive. Without capital punishment, murderers are allowed to participate in and enjoy life.

The U.S. government once followed the example of Germany, Britain, France, and other nations that no longer execute their citizens. However, since 1977, our society **has been allowing** capital punishment again, at a high cost. We cannot imagine the pain of family members who **have been waiting** for years for the government's decision to execute or not execute their loved ones. It also costs the taxpayer millions of dollars more to execute a criminal than to imprison that criminal for life. Prison is a better form of punishment because it protects society and punishes criminals by taking away their freedom.

Present Perfect and Present Perfect Progressive

1. We often use the **present perfect** to talk about an action that started in the past, continues into the present, and may continue into the future.

   - She **has visited** him almost every day.

2. We often use the **present perfect** to indicate that an action is recently completed.

   - Their hopes and plans **have ended** permanently. (Completed action)

3. We often use the **present perfect progressive** to show that an action that began in the past is still continuing.

   - We cannot imagine the pain of family members who **have been waiting** for years for the government's decision to execute or not execute their loved ones. (Continuing action)

4. Non-action verbs, such as *be,* and verbs that refer to mental states or emotions (*believe, wish, trust*), are not used in the present perfect progressive.

   - For most prisoners, life in prison **has been** difficult.

     Many prisoners **have wished** that they could be free.

5. You can use the **present perfect** and the **present perfect progressive** with the time expressions *for* and *since.* Both forms are used with adverbs such as *always* and *recently.*

   - …however, **since** 1977, our society has been allowing capital punishment again …

     We cannot imagine the pain of family members who have been waiting **for** years for the government's decision to execute or not execute their loved ones.

2 *Read this passage, which describes the life of a prisoner. Add the present perfect or the present perfect progressive forms of the verbs in parentheses.*

Wayne Paulson _____ in prison since 1992. For three years he
                        1. (be)

_____ for the government's decision whether or not to execute
 2. (wait)

him. Lately, he _____ letters because he wants to make sure that
                  3. (write)

his loved ones understand that he is innocent. He _____ very
                                                    4. (be)

lonely in prison. Only a few people _____ him. But one person
                                      5. (visit)

_____ to see him nearly every day—his mother. She will visit him

6. (come)

as long as he remains in prison because she _____ that her son is

7. (always/believe)

innocent. Wayne's mother _____ everyone that her son is a good

8. (tell)

citizen. She will continue to do this as often as she can because she

_____ her son since the day he was born.

9. (love)

C WRITING TOPICS

*Choose one of the following topics. Write two or three paragraphs, using some of the
vocabulary, grammar, and style that you learned in this unit.*

1. Imagine that in your local area, capital punishment has been illegal for
   several years. Now the government plans to begin using it again. Write
   a letter to the editor of your local newspaper expressing your opinion of
   capital punishment.

2. Write a letter to Wayne Paulson. Explain what you have learned about the
   question of capital punishment. Give him some advice about what he might
   do in prison to make the best possible use of his time.

3. Discuss whether or not children are punished by society in a culture you
   know well. If so, what kinds of punishment are given? For example, are
   children sent to prison? Do you think it is a good idea to punish children?

4. At times, people who visit foreign countries have trouble with the law. When
   they are punished, they sometimes receive stronger punishments than they
   would in their home countries. Do you believe that certain countries give
   punishments that are too strong?

D RESEARCH TOPICS

Find out about a specific country and its laws relating to the death penalty.
Below are some suggested places:

- Angola, Cambodia, Nepal, Poland, and Moldova are countries which have
  recently abolished the death penalty for either capital crimes or all crimes.

- Gambia, Papua New Guinea, and the Philippines previously abolished the
  death penalty but have reintroduced it.

- Australia, Finland, and Nicaragua do not have the death penalty for any
  crime.

- The United States, Bangladesh, Guatemala, China, Japan, and Uganda
  have capital punishment for capital crimes.

Step 1:   Choose a country. Go to the library to research the history of its death penalty laws.

Step 2:   Answer these questions.

- During what period did the death penalty exist?

- Was it used for all crimes, or was it used only for exceptional crimes such as wartime crimes?

- When was it abolished?

- What is the current situation? For example, does the death penalty still exist, or has it been abolished? If it still exists in the law books, is it being used?

- Are there any plans to change the current death penalty laws? (Note: France has abolished the death penalty, but surveys show that 50 percent of the citizens would support bringing it back.)

Add three questions of your own.

- _____

- _____

- _____

Step 3:   Work in small groups to discuss the information that you found. Write a one- to three-paragraph report to explain what you learned from this fieldwork. Then read your report to the class. You could also have your research published in the school newspaper.

For step-by-step practice in the writing process, see *Writing Activity Book, Intermediate,* Unit 9.

Assignment	Persuasive Essay
Prewriting	Listing
Organizing	Persuading the Reader
Revising	Developing Sentence Variety
	Using the Present Perfect and Present Perfect Progressive
Editing	Punctuating Simple and Compound Sentences

For Unit 9 Internet activities, visit the NorthStar Companion Website at http://www.longman.com/northstar.

Finding a Spouse

1 Focus on the Topic

A PREDICTING

Read the following joke. Then discuss the questions with the class.

Marriage has three rings: an engagement ring, a wedding ring, and suffering.

1. What's the meaning of this joke?

2. In your home culture, do men or women wear wedding or engagement rings? In what other ways do they show that they are engaged or married?

3. Do you agree that suffering is a part of marriage? Why or why not?

B   SHARING INFORMATION

People choose marriage partners for various reasons. Which of the following reasons for choosing a marriage partner is important to you? Mark each one from 1 to 5 (1 = very important; 5 = not important). Then discuss your choices with a partner.

_____   **a.** ability to have children

_____   **b.** partner's age

_____   **c.** parents' choice

_____   **d.** religion

_____   **e.** love

C   PREPARING TO READ

BACKGROUND

Test your knowledge of marriage customs around the world. Choose the culture that you think practices the custom described in each sentence. Write the letter(s) on the line. There may be more than one correct choice.

a. Arab	b. German	c. Native American	d. Vietnamese
e. Chinese	f. Mexican	g. North American	

_____   **1.** Young women often read magazines offering wedding advice.

_____   **2.** Girls are allowed to choose their favorite boy for a husband.

_____   **3.** Young women used to invite men to visit them at night by leaving their windows open.

_____   **4.** Men and women usually decide to get married without any advice from their parents.

_____   **5.** Parents usually choose a marriage partner for their children.

_____   **6.** A man may have more than one wife.

_____   **7.** Marriage partners sometimes do not know each other before their wedding.

VOCABULARY FOR COMPREHENSION

Complete the crossword puzzle. Read the clues on page 177, and choose words from the box.

background	fertility	produce	romantic
characteristics	leadership	raise	spouse
community	pregnancy		

Across

2. The physical condition during which a baby develops inside a woman's body

5. Past experience, including family life and education

6. To take care of children as they grow from babies to adults

7. A group of people who live and work together

8. The ability to direct other people

9. The ability to have children

10. To make or create

Down

1. Related to strong feelings of love between a man and a woman

3. Features or qualities that belong to an animal, person, or object

4. A husband or a wife

2 Focus on Reading

The following article appeared in a journal for students of anthropology (the study of how human beings live together in communities). Read the first paragraph of the article. Then answer the questions.

What about you? If you are already married, how did you find your spouse? If you are single, what do you think is the best way for you to find a spouse?

_____

_____

Finding a Spouse

1   All human beings are born into families, and families begin with the joining together of a man and a woman in marriage. All societies have their own form of marriage. The ideas that we have about marriage are part of our cultural background; they are part of our basic beliefs about right and wrong. As we study marriage, we find that different cultures have solved the problem of finding a spouse in different ways. Finding a marriage partner has never been easy for people, no matter when or where they have lived.

2   In traditional Chinese culture, marriage decisions were made by parents for their children. Parents who wanted to find a spouse for their son or daughter asked a matchmaker to find someone with the right characteristics, including age and educational background. According to the Chinese way of thinking, it would be a serious mistake to allow two young people to follow their romantic feelings and choose their own partners. The all-important decision of marriage was made by older family members, who understood that the goal of marriage was to produce healthy sons. In traditional Chinese society, sons were important because they would take positions of leadership in the family and keep the family name alive.

3   As part of our cultural background, beliefs about marriage can be as different as the cultures of the world. While the traditional Chinese did not believe that young people should be free to choose their own marriage partners, the Hopi, a native people of North America, had a very different idea about freedom. The Hopi allowed boys to leave their parents' home at age thirteen to live in a *kiva,* a special home for young males. Here they enjoyed the freedom to go out alone at night and secretly visit young girls. Most boys tried to leave the girl's home before daylight, but a girl's parents usually did not get angry about the night visits. They allowed the visits to continue if they thought the boy was someone who would make a good marriage partner. After a few months of receiving visits, most girls became pregnant. As a consequence, they could choose their favorite boy for a husband.

4   The Hopi culture is not the only one that allowed young people to visit each other at night. Some Bavarian people of southern Germany once had a "windowing" custom that took place when young women left their windows open at night so that young men could enter their bedrooms. When a woman became pregnant, the man usually asked her to marry him. But women who did not get pregnant after windowing were often unable to find a husband. This was because fertility was a very important requirement for women in this culture, and the windowing custom allowed them to prove their fertility to others in the community. Some people are surprised when they learn of this unique custom because they expect the people of southern Germany to follow the rules of the Catholic religion, which teach that it is wrong for unmarried women to become pregnant. But the windowing custom is only one example of the surprising views of marriage that are found around the world, even among people whose religious beliefs require more common marriage practices.

5   One view of marriage that surprises most of us today was held by John Noyes, a religious man who started the Oneida Community in the state of New York in 1831. He began it as an experiment of a different way of living. Noyes decided that group marriage was the best way for men and women to live together. In this form of marriage, men and women changed partners frequently. They were expected to love all members of the community equally. Children belonged to all members of the community, and all the adults worked hard to support themselves and shared everything they had. Members of the Oneida Community lived this lifestyle for a while without any serious problems; however, this way of life ended when John Noyes left the community in 1876. Without his leadership and unique way of thinking, members of the community quickly returned to the traditional marriage of one woman and one man.

6   A more famous example of a different style of marriage is found among the early Mormons. The group's first leader, Joseph Smith, believed that a man should be allowed to have several wives. As the Mormon Church grew, many of the men followed Smith's teaching and married a number of wives. The Mormons believed that it was a woman's duty to marry at a young age and raise as many children as possible. For example, in 1854, one Mormon leader became a father nine times in one week when nine of his wives all had babies. Today the Mormon Church, which calls itself the Church of Jesus Christ of Latter-Day Saints, teaches that marriage should be a partnership of one man and one woman who will be together not only during this life, but forever.

7   In these modern times, there are some men who might agree with the custom of allowing a man to have as many wives as he chooses. Many young lovers today dream of the freedom of the Hopi, and some of us wish that a matchmaker would help us find the perfect mate. Finding a spouse with whom we can commit to spending a lifetime has always been an important concern. Despite all the different ways of finding a marriage partner, one idea is the same throughout the world: Marriage is a basic and important part of human life.

READING FOR MAIN IDEAS

The following sentences describe cultural beliefs. Match each belief to the culture in which it exists.

a. Hopi   b. Bavarian   c. Oneida Community   d. Chinese   e. Mormon

_____ 1. Young people are not capable of making the right marriage choices for themselves.

_____ 2. Getting pregnant shows that you will be a good wife.

_____ 3. Women should get married as early in their lives as possible.

_____ 4. A girl should be free to choose her own husband.

_____ 5. It is better for society if people are not limited to one marriage partner.

READING FOR DETAILS

Briefly answer the following questions. Then check your answers with a partner.

1. Who helped Chinese parents choose a spouse for their sons or daughters? How did this person help?

   _____

2. What was the Chinese idea of a successful marriage?

   _____

3. Why did Hopi parents sometimes stop night visits?

   _____

4. What do people in some Catholic countries believe about unmarried women?

   _____

5. What did John Noyes believe about marriage?

_____

6. How has the Mormon idea of marriage changed?

_____

REACTING TO THE READING

1 *Identify the culture in which each of the following problems could be taking place. Describe the cultural belief that may relate to the problem.*

Example

A girl cannot marry the boy she loves because another girl has already chosen him for a husband.

Culture: _Hopi_____

Cultural Belief: _It's a good idea to let girls choose who they want for a_____

_husband._____

1. A husband is upset because his wife has given birth to another daughter.

   Culture: _____

   Cultural Belief: _____

2. A woman is very jealous of her best friend because she is pregnant.

   Culture: _____

   Cultural Belief: _____

3. A man doesn't want his wife to love another man, but he is afraid to tell her how he feels.

   Culture: _____

   Cultural Belief: _____

4. Two sisters hope to marry the same man so that they can still live together after they get married.

   Culture: _____

   Cultural Belief: _____

5. Two young lovers wish they could spend their lives together, but they cannot.

Culture: _____

Cultural Belief: _____

6. A girl and her parents are fighting because her parents don't want the boy she loves to see her.

Culture: _____

Cultural Belief: _____

2 *Consider the following points from the text about finding a spouse:*

- arranged by parents
- girls choosing their favorite boy after becoming pregnant
- the "windowing" custom
- group marriage
- one man having multiple wives

Discuss with a classmate the pros and cons of each way of finding a spouse. Which way do you like the most? the least?

Write a paragraph below giving your opinion of the best way to find a spouse. Share your paragraph with the class.

_____

_____

_____

_____

_____

_____

_____

_____

_____

_____

_____

_____

B   READING TWO: *What's Wrong with Tradition?*

The following letter appeared in the student newspaper of an American university. It was written by an international student who believes strongly in his country's traditional way of choosing spouses.

Letter to the Editor

Dear Editor:

1   I am a twenty-seven-year-old student from Vietnam. My purpose in coming here is to get a business degree. I am very grateful to have the chance to get an education in a country of such great business leadership. However, I am tired of the questions that people ask me about my personal life. American students seem to think that their way of dating romantically before marriage is the only way, but I disagree. Let me give you an example from my own life.

2   My parents have been married for thirty-five years. Their marriage has all the characteristics of a happy one: deep friendship, love, and trust. They have six children, and I am the second son. Because of their help, I am able to study in the United States. They have always worked hard to raise their children in the right way. When I finish my degree, I will go back to my country and help them.

3   American people are always surprised when I tell them that my parents met for the first time on their wedding day. Americans can't believe that such a marriage could be happy, but I have seen my parents with my own eyes. They love each other faithfully, and they are proud of the children that their marriage has produced. They learned to love each other slowly, as time passed. I believe they share a true and everlasting love.

4   When people ask, "Are you looking for a girlfriend?" I tell them no. For me, studying comes first. When I go back to my country and start working, my parents will help me find a good wife. She will be someone with a good family background, someone I can trust. Good apples come from good trees. If I marry a good apple, we can make a beautiful, growing tree together: no divorce, no AIDS, no broken heart.

5   I want a peaceful, happy life just like my parents have. Why can't Americans understand this?

Paul Nguyen

Write your response to Paul Nguyen's letter in the space below. Then share what you have written with the class.

Dear Paul Nguyen,

   I am writing in response to your letter that appeared in the student newspaper. I would like to share my opinion with you. I believe that _____

_____

_____. This is because

_____

_____. I also have a

question for you. _____

_____

_____? In my opinion, _____

_____

_____.

   Thank you for allowing me to share my thoughts.

                              Sincerely,

                    _____

C   LINKING READINGS ONE AND TWO

Discuss these questions in small groups.

1. Paul Nguyen explains that his parents met on their wedding day. Who do you think made the decision for this couple to get married?

2. Consider your own parents. When did they meet? How did they meet? Who made the decision for them to get married?

3. Look at the number line below. According to what you learned in Readings
   One and Two, give each of the following cultures a number from the graph.
   Discuss your choices in small groups.

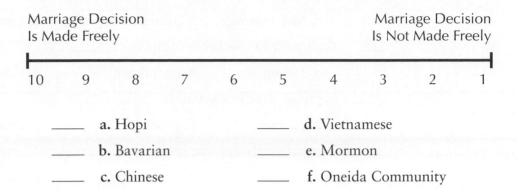

Marriage Decision   Marriage Decision
Is Made Freely   Is Not Made Freely

10   9   8   7   6   5   4   3   2   1

_____ **a.** Hopi   _____ **d.** Vietnamese

_____ **b.** Bavarian   _____ **e.** Mormon

_____ **c.** Chinese   _____ **f.** Oneida Community

3 Focus on Vocabulary

1 *Review the list of analogy types, their definitions, and the examples. Then analyze the
relationships among the vocabulary words. Choose the word that best completes the
analogy, and circle it. Be sure that the second pair of words has a similar relationship to
the first pair of words. Label each analogy to identify type. The first one has been done
for you.*

Analogy Types	Definitions	Examples
Synonym (**S**)	The words have a very similar meaning.	mistake : error
Antonym (**A**)	The words have opposite meanings.	modern : traditional
Cause/effect (**C/E**)	One word is the result of another word.	mistakes : experience
Degree (**D**)	One word has a stronger meaning than the other.	different : unique
Related (**R**)	The words are connected by similar ideas.	tough : suffering

_S_ **1.** characteristics : features = make : _____

    a. raise   (**b.** produce)   **c.** grow

_____ **2.** spouse : husband = romantic : _____

    a. characteristic   **b.** infertility   **c.** attracted to

_____ 3. marriage : divorce = pregnancy : _____

    a. infertility   **b.** commitment   **c.** traditional

_____ 4. pregnancy : baby = romance : _____

    a. love marriage   **b.** arranged marriage   **c.** group marriage

_____ 5. surprised : shocked = enduring : _____

    a. lasting   **b.** continuing   **c.** everlasting

_____ 6. group : leader = marriage : _____

    a. partner   **b.** produce   **c.** characteristics

_____ 7. usually : always = neighbor : _____

    a. friend   **b.** community   **c.** boss

_____ 8. engagement : marriage = fertility : _____

    a. miracle   **b.** proof   **c.** pregnancy

2 *Read the information below about courtship. Then decide if the following sentences are related to courtship (**C**), a wedding ceremony (**W**), or married life (**M**). Write the appropriate letter next to each sentence. Then put the sentences in a time order that makes sense. Write a number next to each sentence. Share your choices with the class.*

Courtship refers to the period of time when a man and a woman get to know each other before marriage. In some cultures, they spend time together alone. In other cultures, they spend time together with friends and relatives. During this time, a couple may decide whether or not to marry.

_____   **a.** Members of the community are invited to watch the couple promise to love each other for a lifetime.

_____   **b.** The man gives the woman flowers to show his romantic feelings for the first time.

_____   **c.** The husband and wife disagree about the best way to raise their two sons.

_____   **d.** Friends and relatives throw rice at the couple to make a wish for their fertility.

_____   **e.** The husband and wife hope that their marriage will produce healthy children.

C-1   **f.** A man and a woman are attracted to each other because of such characteristics as good looks, intelligence, and kindness.

_____   **g.** Important words are spoken by a person in a position of leadership.

_____ **h.** The woman happily tells her mother that she is pregnant.

_____ **i.** The man realizes that the woman will be an excellent spouse.

_____ **j.** Little by little, each partner discovers more about the other's background.

3 *Describe a courtship tradition in your culture. Write one or two paragraphs using at least five of the words below. Or, describe five different courtship traditions in your culture using five of the words below.*

background	produce	romantic	spouse
unique	prove	traditional	opportunity
characteristics	fertility	community	modern

4 Focus on Writing

A   STYLE: Using Related Word Forms for Cohesion

1 *In a well-written text, the ideas are cohesive; that is, they fit together clearly. The word for this clear, fitting together of ideas is* **cohesion.** *Look at the following paragraphs about marriage. Can you identify what makes them cohesive?*

a. Some people are surprised when they learn of this unique custom because they expect the people of southern Germany to follow the rules of the Catholic religion, which teach that it is wrong for unmarried women to become pregnant. But the windowing custom is only one example of the surprising views of marriage that are found around the world, even among people whose religious beliefs require more common marriage practices.

b. A more famous example of a different style of marriage is found among the early Mormons. The group's first leader, Joseph Smith, believed that a man should be allowed to have several wives. As the Mormon Church grew, many of the men followed Smith's teaching and married a number of wives. The Mormons believed that it was a woman's duty to marry at a young age and raise as many children as possible. For example, in 1854, one Mormon leader became a father nine times in one week when nine of his wives all had babies. Today the Mormon Church teaches that marriage should be a partnership of one man and one woman who will be together not only during this life, but forever.

Writers use related word forms to gain more **cohesion** in their writing. In paragraph **a,** the ideas fit together clearly because the writer uses such related word forms as *religion* and *religious, unmarried* and *marriage.* In paragraph **b,** some related word forms are *marriage, married,* and *marry.* There are also many repetitions of the words *Mormon* and *wives.* The use of related word forms helps the writer move smoothly from one idea to the next. The writer is able to keep the reader's focus on the main idea without repeating the same exact words again and again. Look at the following example:

> Other pregnant women believe that they are quite **beautiful** during pregnancy. Their **beauty** comes from the joy of becoming a mother. There is a light in their eyes, and their skin shines **beautifully.**

2 *Complete the paragraph below with the appropriate word forms. Choose from the box.*

romance	married	similar	traditional	courtship
tradition	court	romantic	marriage	similarity

Many social scientists agree that it is important to marry someone whose

background is _____ (1) to your own. One example of this idea is

expressed when Americans talk about marrying "the boy (or girl) next door."

When we get _____ (2) to the boy or girl next door, we are joining

our lives with a partner who shares our lifestyle, income, and educational level.

According to social scientists, this type of _____ (3) is likely to

be successful because the spouses will understand each other more easily.

One practical advantage of marrying the boy or girl next door is that it is

easy to _____ (4) someone who lives near you. During the

_____ (5) period, the two partners can get together easily. If they

come from _____ (6) families, their parents can watch their

relationship develop and give them advice. Of course, there is also the possibility

that the _____ (7) will not be accepted by parents, and the young

couple may not be able to participate in the _____ of having
(8)

a wedding ceremony. They may elope, or run away to get married secretly. For

some couples, this is a _____ way to begin their lives together. But
(9)

whether or not they elope, many experts believe that people who marry the boy

or girl next door will be happy. This is because of the _____ of
(10)

their backgrounds.

B   GRAMMAR: Articles—Definite and Indefinite

1 *Look at the following passage from "Finding a Spouse." Underline the indefinite article*
a. *Circle the definite article* **the.** *How are these articles different in meaning?*

A more famous example of a different style of marriage is found among the
early Mormons. The group's first leader, Joseph Smith, believed that a man
should be allowed to have several wives. As the Mormon Church grew, many of
the men followed Smith's teaching and married a number of wives. The Mormons
believed that it was a woman's duty to marry at a young age and raise as many
children as possible. For example, in 1854, one Mormon leader became a father
nine times in one week when nine of his wives all had babies. Today the Mormon
Church . . . teaches that marriage should be a partnership of one man and one
woman who will be together not only during this life but also forever.

Articles: Definite and Indefinite

1. Use the definite article ***the*** when you have a particular person, place, or thing in mind.	**The** group's first leader, Joseph Smith, believed that a man should be allowed to have several wives.
	As **the** Mormon Church grew, many of **the** men followed Smith's teaching and married a number of wives.
2. Use the indefinite article ***a*** when you do not have a particular person, place, or thing in mind. Use the indefinite article ***an*** before words that begin with vowel sounds.	The group's first leader, Joseph Smith, believed that **a** man should be allowed to have several wives.

(continued)

3. Use the indefinite article **a** the first time you mention a person, place, or thing. Then use the definite article **the** when you refer to that same thing again.

Some Bavarian people of southern Germany once had **a** "windowing" custom that …

…and **the** windowing custom allowed them to prove their fertility to others in the community.

4. Use the definite article **the** in forming the superlative of an adjective.

Noyes decided that group marriage was **the** best way for men and women to live together.

2 *Complete the paragraph below with the indefinite article* **a(n)** *or the definite article* **the.**

Planning a Wedding

The American bride often looks in _____ bridal magazine for advice
(1)

about planning her wedding. Every bride has her own idea of _____ most
(2)

perfect wedding. For most brides, this includes flowers, music, and _____
(3)

delicious wedding cake. Most magazines also provide information about

planning _____ romantic trip. Some brides dream of going to _____
(4)   (5)

warm beach, while others wish to travel to _____ distant country. Bridal
(6)

magazines also give advice about following traditional American wedding

customs. For example, _____ bride will sometimes give _____ piece of
(7)   (8)

wedding cake to her friends. Each friend takes _____ piece of cake home
(9)

and places it in a bag underneath her pillow. According to tradition, if a woman

does this, she will dream of her future husband at night. _____ woman will
(10)

see his face in her dreams.

C   WRITING TOPICS

Choose one of the following topics. Write two or three paragraphs, using some of the grammar, vocabulary, and style that you learned in this unit.

1. What are the characteristics of a good spouse? Give examples to support your opinion.

2. What are the characteristics of a happy marriage? Do these characteristics change with the passing of time? Or do they remain the same?

3. Do you believe that using a matchmaker can be a good way to find a spouse? Why or why not?

4. Describe a marriage or courtship custom with which you are familiar. Is this custom related to religion? Explain.

D   RESEARCH TOPICS

Step 1: Look at several newspapers and magazines. How much information can you find that is related to courtship and marriage? Use the questions below to organize the information that you find.

1. How many wedding announcements did you find? _____

2. How many of the following types of advertisements did you find?
   - matchmaking services _____
   - wedding fashions/jewelry _____
   - honeymoon travel _____
   - other: _____

     (Describe): _____

3. How many articles did you find? _____

4. How much marriage advice did you find in advice columns*? _____

Step 2: Use the following questions as a guide to write a short summary of your research. Share your summary with the class.

   - Which articles were the most interesting? Why?

(continued)

---

* *advice columns:* a special section in a newspaper where people ask for and get advice

- What kind of advertisements did you see most often? Did these advertisements make you want to buy the product or service?

- What kind of problems did you find in the advice columns? Were any of these problems related to information in this unit? Explain.

For step-by-step practice in the writing process, see *Writing Activity Book, Intermediate,* Unit 10.

Assignment	Descriptive Essay
Prewriting	Categorizing
Organizing	Using Point-by-Point Organization
Revising	Using Related Word Forms for Cohesion
	Choosing Definite or Indefinite Articles
Editing	Reviewing Punctuation

For Unit 10 Internet activities, visit the NorthStar Companion Website at http://longman.com/northstar.

Grammar Book References

NorthStar: Reading and Writing, Intermediate, Second Edition	Focus on Grammar 3, Third Edition	Azar's Fundamentals of English Grammar, Third Edition
Unit 1 Contrast—Simple Present and Present Progressive	**Unit 1** Present Progressive and Simple Present	**Chapter 1** The Simple Present and the Present Progressive: 1-1
Unit 2 Modals of Ability	**Unit 11** Ability: *Can, Could, Be able to*	**Chapter 7** Expressing Ability: *Can* and *Could:* 7-2
Unit 3 Adjectives—Superlatives	**Unit 25** Adjective: Superlatives	**Chapter 9** Comparative and Superlative: 9-2 Comparative and Superlative Forms of Adjectives and Adverbs: 9-3
Unit 4 Infinitives of Purpose	**Unit 30** Infinitives of Purpose	**Chapter 13** Expressing Purpose with *In order to* and *For:* 13-9
Unit 5 Using Modals for Requests	**Unit 13** Requests: *Can, Could, Will, Would, Would you mind*	**Chapter 7** Polite Questions: *May I, Could I, Can I:* 7-5 Polite Questions: *Would you, Could you, Will you, Can you:* 7-6
Unit 6 Past Progressive and Simple Past	**Unit 4** Past Progressive and Simple Past	**Chapter 2** The Simple Past and the Past Progressive: 2-8

NorthStar: Reading and Writing, Intermediate, Second Edition	Focus on Grammar 3, Third Edition	Azar's Fundamentals of English Grammar, Third Edition
Unit 7 Noun Clauses with *Wh*-words	**Unit 8** *Wh-* Questions: Subject and Object	**Chapter 14** Noun Clauses That Begin with a Question Word: 14-2 Noun Clauses with *Who, What, Whose + Be:* 14-3
Unit 8 Describing the Past with *Used to*	**Unit 5** *Used to*	**Chapter 2** Expressing Past Habit: *Used to:* 2-11 **Chapter 10** *Used to* vs. *Be used to:* 10-11
Unit 9 Contrast—Present Perfect and Present Perfect Progressive	**Unit 20** Present Perfect Progressive and Present Perfect	**Chapter 4** Forms of the Present Perfect: 4-2 Present Perfect Progressive: 4-6 Present Perfect Progressive vs. Present Perfect: 4-7
Unit 10 Articles—Definite and Indefinite	**Unit 22** Articles: Indefinite and Definite	**Chapter 11** Count/Noncount Nouns and Articles

Credits

Photo credits: Page **1** The Quaker Oats Company; **4** Eveready Battery Company, Inc.; **19** Peter Grumann/Getty Images; **22** Duomo/Corbis; **29** Bettmann/Corbis; **53** Raymond A. Mendez/Animals Animals; **54** Bettmann/Corbis; **77** Peter Cade/Getty Images; **96** Roger Mear/Getty Images; **100** George Lepp/Getty Images; **113** Photofest; **122** Photofest; **135** Corbis; **151** H. F. Davis/Getty Images; **155** UPI/Corbis Bettmann; **175** Dave Bartruff/Corbis; **178** AP/Wide World Photos.

Illustration credits: Hal Just, p. 93; Paul McCusker, p. 114.

Text credits: p. 22: This imaginary interview was created by the authors using published information from *Hawk Occupation: Skateboarder* by Tony Hawk with Sean Mortimer, copyright 2001. Regan Books, p. 118: Information from this passage was taken from *Love, Lucy* by Lucille Ball, copyright 1997. Berkley Publishing Group.

Reviewers

Lubie G. Alatriste, Lehman College; **A. Morgan Andaluz,** Leeward Community College; **Chris Antonellis,** Boston University CELOP; **Christine Baez,** Universidad de las Américas, Mexico City, Mexico; **Betty Baron,** Johnson County Community College; **Rudy Besikof,** University of California San Diego; **Mary Black,** Institute of North American Studies; **Dorothy Buroh,** University of California, San Diego; **Kay Caldwell,** Leeward Community College; **Margarita Canales;** Universidad Latinoamericana, Mexico City, Mexico; **Jose Carvalho,** University of Massachusetts Boston; **Philip R. Condorelli,** University of Massachusetts Boston; **Pamela Couch,** Boston University CELOP; **Barbara F. Dingee,** University of Massachusetts Boston; **Jeanne M. Dunnet,** Central Connecticut State University; **Samuela Eckstut-Didier,** Boston University CELOP; Patricia Hedden, Yonsei University; **Hostos Community College; GEOS Language Institute;** Jennifer M. Gerrity, University of Massachusetts Boston; **Lis Jenkinson,** Northern Virginia Community College; **Glenna Jennings,** University of California, San Diego; **Diana Jones,** Instituto Angloamericano, Mexico City, Mexico; **Matt Kaeiser,** Old Dominion University; **Regina Kandraska,** University of Massachusetts Boston; **King Fahd University of Petroleum & Minerals; Chris Ko,** Kyang Hee University; **Charalambos Kollias,** The Hellenic-American Union; **Barbara Kruchin,** Columbia University ALP; **Language Training Institute;** Jacqueline LoConde, Boston University CELOP; **Mary Lynch,** University of Massachusetts Boston; **Julia Paranionova,** Moscow State Pedagogical University; **Pasadena City College; Pontifical Xavier University;** Natalya Morozova, Moscow State Pedagogical University; **Mary Carole Ramiowski,** University of Seoul; Jon Robinson, University of Seoul; **Michael Sagliano,** Leeward Community College; **Janet Shanks,** Columbia University ALP; **Eric Tejeda;** PROULEX, Guadalajara, Mexico; **Truman College; United Arab Emirates University; University of Minnesota; Karen Whitlow,** Johnson County Community College

Notes

Notes

Notes

Notes

Notes

Notes

Notes

Notes

Notes

Notes

Notes